A practical guide

ARTIFICIAL BREEDING OF CATTLE

Dennis Boothby
Geoff Fahey

Published by Halstead Press
19a Boundary St.,
Rushcutters Bay, N.S.W. 2011

First published in 1995 by Agmedia, Melbourne.
Halstead edition, Sydney, 2000.

© Copyright 1995: State of Queensland, Department of Primary Industries.
Not to be copied in whole or part without authority.
Printed by Australian Print Group, Maryborough, Vic.

National Library cataloguing in publication entry

Boothby, Dennis, 1949—.
  Artificial breeding of cattle: a practical guide.

  Bibliography.
  Includes index.
  ISBN 1 875684 50 6

  1. Cattle - Artificial insemination. 2. Cattle - Breeding.
  II. Fahey, Geoff. II. Agmedia. III. Title.

  636.208245

The information in this book is of a general nature and the contents do not take into account all the factors which affect practical implementation in each circumstance. Accordingly it is not to be relied on as a substititute for specific advice.

TABLE OF CONTENTS

Preface 5

Introduction 6

Chapter 1 – Reproductive Tract of the Cow 8

Chapter 2 – Physiology of Reproduction of the Cow 11

    The Oestrous Cycle and Hormones 11

    Fertilisation 16

    Pregnancy and Parturition 19

Chapter 3 – Anatomy and Physiology of the Bull 26

Chapter 4 – Semen – Collection, Processing and Storage 31

    AB Centre Operations 31

    Liquid Nitrogen Containers 39

Chapter 5 – Insemination Technique 46

    Semen Handling 46

    Insemination of the Cow 52

    Hygiene 57

    Faults in AI Technique 58

Chapter 6 – Bull Selection 63

    Basic Genetics 63

    Dairy Bulls Selection – Progeny Testing and ABVs 67

    Beef Bull Selection –

        Performance Recording and Analysis 73

Chapter 7 – Conducting an AB Program   81
        Oestrus Detection Methods   81

        Oestrus Synchronisation   88

        Planning and Preparation   94

Chapter 8 – Breeding Records –

    the Basis of Sound Management   102

Chapter 9 – Factors Affecting Reproduction   110

        Nutrition   110

        Diseases of Reproduction   113

Chapter 10 – Uses of Artificial Breeding   116

Glossary   121

PREFACE

This book is designed to facilitate the training of cattle breeders to artificially inseminate cows and as a detailed source of information about all facets of cattle breeding and reproductive management for cattle producers, educational institutions, extension officers and veterinarians.

Dennis Boothby is a veterinarian based at Beef Breeding Services, Artificial Breeding Centre, at Wacol, near Brisbane. Geoff Fahey is a beef extension specialist with Beef Breeding Services at Gympie. Both authors currently work for the Queensland Department of Primary Industries and have extensive experience in both the beef and dairy industries, including training beef and dairy producers in artificial insemination. Collectively they have trained some 8000 cattle producers in Queensland, New South Wales, Western Australia and South East Asia.

Dennis Boothby QDAH, BVSc
Geoff Fahey QCAH, Assoc Dip Farm Man, Dip Mar Res, BBus

INTRODUCTION

AI (artificial insemination), also known as AB (artificial breeding), is the physical placement of semen into the reproductive tract of females with the aim of achieving pregnancies by means other than that of natural mating.

AI is not new. It was recorded as early as the 14th century when it was reputedly used by an Arabian horse breeder, who transferred the contents of an ejaculate from the vagina of a freshly served mare into the vagina of another mare by means of a sponge.

Detailed knowledge of the physiology of reproduction commenced in 1677 when the Dutch scientist, Van Loenhoek, observed sperm cells in an ejaculate. The first scientific artificial breeding was done with drugs in 1780, by an Italian physiologist, Spallanzani, who proved that the sperm fraction of the ejaculate is the component which causes fertilisation.

Serious efforts to promote artificial insemination of cattle were made in Russia in 1914 by Ivanov and his co-workers, who developed the artificial vagina (AV) to facilitate semen collection from bulls. This was followed by experimentation with insemination procedures and methods of diluting semen. By using AI they hoped to restrict the spread of vibriosis—a venereal disease of cattle.

In 1937 AI in cattle became a practical commercial proposition when Sorensen, a Danish veterinarian, and his co-workers, developed the recto-vaginal technique of insemination: the method used worldwide today, and described in this book.

AI spread around the world after a British scientist, Polge, developed techniques for deep freezing of sperm for long term storage in 1949. In France during the 1960s, Cassou brought semen processing technology to its present level by designing the straw system of packaging deep frozen semen, culminating in the development of the mini-straw in 1969. Advances in storage containers using liquid nitrogen as a refrigerant were concurrent with the development and spread of the Cassou straw. The Cassou straw system has been almost universally adopted with more than 200 countries using it as a method of semen packaging.

Many millions of cows throughout the world are bred by AI each year and the number is increasing. In Australia approximately 1·5 million cows are inseminated annually. Most of cows inseminated worldwide are dairy cows, but increasingly AI is being used in the beef industry. AI is the cheapest, safest and most efficient means of spreading superior genetic material and both the beef and dairy cattle industries depend on it for their genetic advancement schemes.

The most recent advances are in the area of oestrous synchronisation. Semen processing advances hoped for in the near future include the sexing of sperm, and slow release sperm capsules.

MORE INFORMATION. Some states and countries have local regulations governing the use of artificial insemination. It is necessary to contact your local department of agriculture, private veterinarian or herd improvement organisation concerning the particular requirements of local legislation. These organisations will also be able to direct you to the local suppliers of AI equipment, semen and training courses that you may require.

THE REPRODUCTIVE TRACT OF THE COW

A sound knowledge of the location, structure and function of the reproductive organs is essential for efficient insemination and for avoiding damage to cows.

EXTERNAL ORGANS. The anus is a ring of muscle which retains the contents of the rectum. Below the anus are the lips of the vulva, the external opening of the vagina.

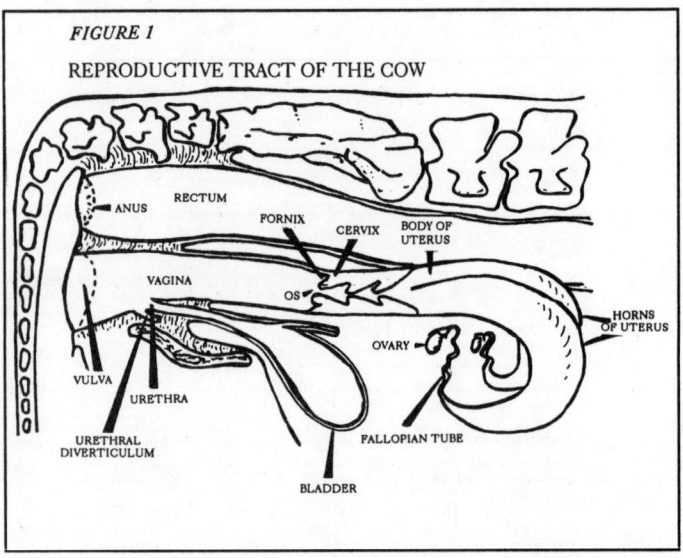

FIGURE 1
REPRODUCTIVE TRACT OF THE COW

PER RECTUM EXAMINATION. The various parts of the reproductive tract can be located by hand, palpating through the elastic wall of the rectum. An arm length glove should be worn for protection and hygiene. For ease of entry, lubricate the gloved hand with obstetric lubricant and form the fingers and thumb into a cone.

INTERNAL ORGANS. The **vagina** is 24 to 30 cm long with muscular walls. About 10 cm inside the vagina along its floor is the passage from the bladder, the urethra. It enters the vagina near a blind pouch, the urethral diverticulum.

The **cervix** is 3 to 10 cm long and from 1·5 to 6 cm in diameter. It is larger in *Bos indicus* animals (Brahman, Zebu and related breeds) than other breeds and increases in size with age. It connects the vagina to the uterus. It is quite firm in comparison with other parts of the tract and can usually be located by feeling gently around the pelvic floor.

The position of the cervix will vary with the age of the cow and the stage of pregnancy. In non-pregnant cows, most operators should not have to go in beyond elbow length to locate the cervix and the rest of the reproductive tract. In heifers, the cervix should be picked up at wrist depth. It may be pulled out of reach by the weight of the developing foetus in a pregnant animal.

A narrow canal passes through the centre of the cervix. It is spiral in form and tightly closed. It opens slightly when the cow is on heat and enlarges greatly during calving. The start of this canal is the os which extends into the vagina forming a blind pocket—the fornix.

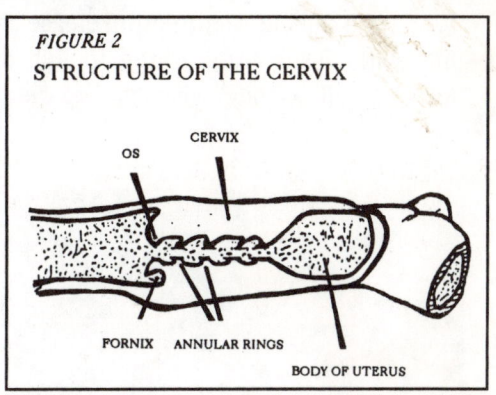

FIGURE 2
STRUCTURE OF THE CERVIX

The **uterus** consists of a body and two horns. The body is 2 to 3 cm long and separates into the horns. The body feels longer on palpation than 2 to 3 cm, because the horns are joined together by a ligament for about 12 cm beyond the point of division.

The two horns are 35 to 40 cm long and 2 cm or more in diameter. They have a thick elastic wall and a rich blood supply to nourish the developing calf.

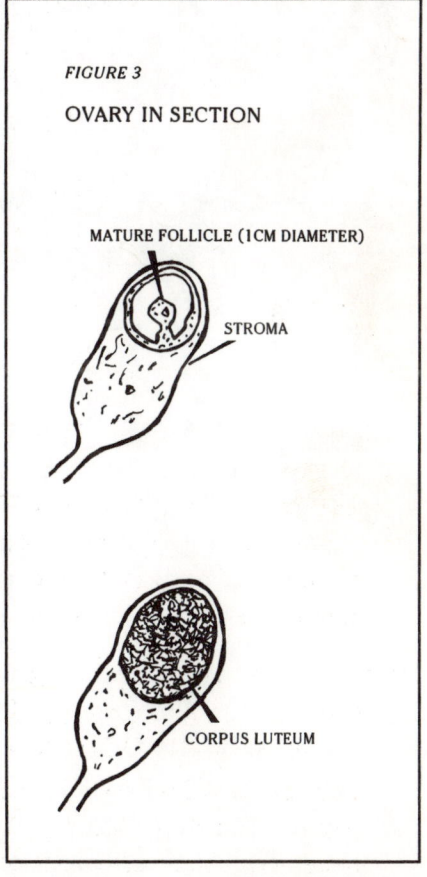

FIGURE 3
OVARY IN SECTION

To imagine the uterus, partly fill a rubber glove with water and run your hand over the start of the join of two fingers. This is approximately the size, shape and consistency of the uterus in the non-pregnant heifer. The ligament may be felt with practice by hooking a finger under it. This may be used to help to retract the uterus into the pelvic cavity. In heifers, muscular contractions of the uterus may cause it to curl up in the operator's hand if gentle palpation is attempted. This makes definition of the structures easier.

The **oviduct** is also known as the fallopian tube. It is 20 to 25 cm long and 1 to 2 mm in diameter. It runs from the tip of the horn to the infundibulum (or funnel) which surrounds the ovary. The oviduct is difficult to detect on palpation. Fertilisation takes place in the oviduct.

10 * THE REPRODUCTIVE TRACT OF THE COW

Ovaries can normally be felt alongside the uterine horns. They are oval in shape with size depending on age and breed (usually the size of an almond nut or slightly larger).

Eggs develop in follicles (fluid filled blisters) below the surface of the ovary. Near the time of ovulation, the follicle will be about one centimetre in diameter.

When the follicle ruptures to release the egg, it leaves a depression which soon fills with tissue. After three to five days this tissue develops into the corpus luteum (yellow body) which an experienced operator can detect by palpation.

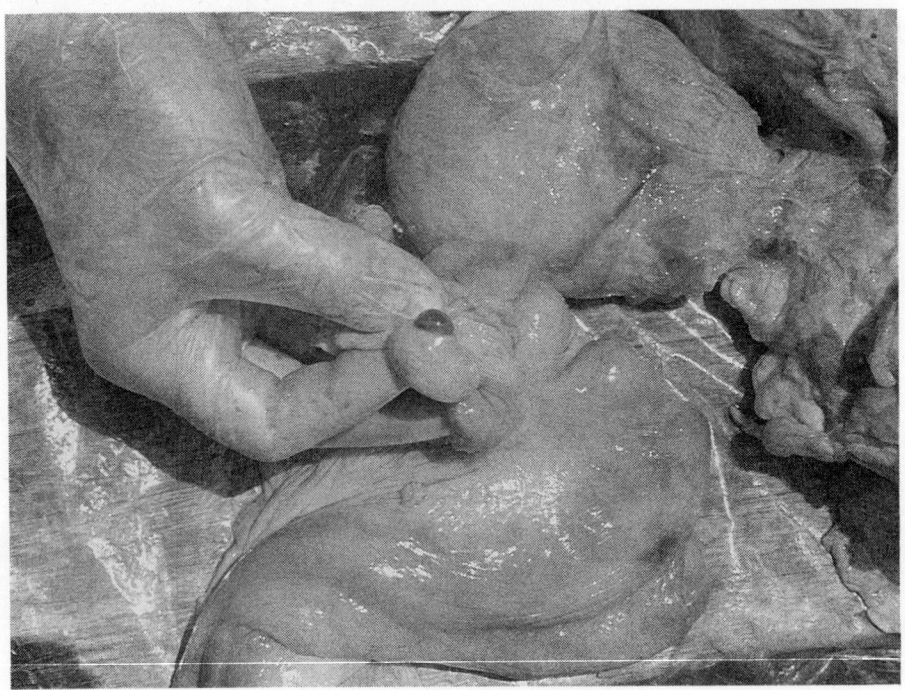

THE CORPUS LUTEUM VISIBLE ON AN OVARY. THIS IS PALPABLE DURING RECTAL EXAMINATION.

PHYSIOLOGY OF REPRODUCTION OF THE COW

The Oestrous Cycle and Hormones

When a heifer becomes sexually mature the ovaries begin to function in a cycle of activity. This cycle involves a sequence of events in preparation for mating, conception and pregnancy. The cycle repeats in preparation for a new mating cycle if pregnancy does not occur.

The cycle has an average length of 21 days. Any period between 18 and 24 days is considered normal.

Stages of Oestrous Cycle

1. OESTRUS (STANDING HEAT, SEXUAL DESIRE)

This is the period of sexual activity at the end of the cycle when the female will stand to permit mating. The duration of oestrus varies within a normal range of 6 to 30 hours. The average duration is:

for heifers	12 hours
for cows	18 hours

2. MET-OESTRUS (AFTER HEAT)

Days 1 to 5 of the cycle. The female will not permit mounting. About 50% of cows and 90% of heifers show met-oestral bleeding. Ovulation occurs during this time and the corpus luteum begins to develop.

> *Met-oestral bleeding* does *not indicate* that the cow has conceived, or not conceived, nor the sex of the calf, nor anything else in particular.

3. DI-OESTRUS (BETWEEN HEATS)

Days 5 to 19. Characterised by a complete lack of sexual desire. If the cow conceives she passes from di-oestrus into a state of anoestrus (absence of cycling).

4. PRO-OESTRUS (BEFORE HEAT)

Days 19 to 21. This is the period of preparation for sexual activity.

ANOESTRUS. Anoestrus is a complete lack of cycling activity. It can occur due to pregnancy, the stress of lactation or poor nutritional status.

Control of the Oestrous Cycle

All stages in the reproductive cycle are controlled by hormones. The term hormone is derived from a word meaning to set in motion or to arouse. Hormones are chemical messengers released from endocrine (ductless) glands. They travel via the blood stream to have an effect on distant target organs. An example of a hormone is adrenalin. It is produced by the adrenal gland situated near the kidney. Release of adrenalin into the bloodstream causes increased heart rate and breathing capacity. When you get a fright it is adrenalin which makes your heart jump.

Hormones Involved in the Reproductive Cycle

Reproduction, like most bodily functions, is controlled from the brain. It exercises this control through a small gland — the pituitary gland — situated immediately beneath the brain. The pituitary gland has two parts, the anterior (towards the front) and the posterior, each producing distinct hormones.

The brain receives messages and stimuli from all parts of the body and from the environment. It acts like a computer and collates these signals. Providing enough signals are favourable, it releases GnRH (gonadotrophin releasing hormone) which causes the pituitary gland to commence the reproductive cycle. Adverse signals such as poor body condition, diseases and stress will cause lowering or cessation of cycling.

STAGE 1–PRO-OESTRUS. Follicle stimulating hormone (FSH) is released from the anterior pituitary gland upon release of GnRH from the brain. FSH acts upon the germinal epithelium of the ovary to cause the formation of the follicle (the 'Graafian follicle') containing the ovum.

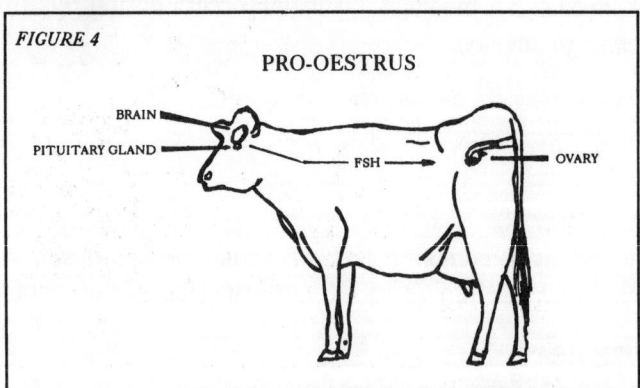

FIGURE 4 — PRO-OESTRUS

STAGE 2–OESTRUS. The fluid in the follicle contains much oestrogen. Oestrogen is the female hormone, which is produced continuously in small quantities in the cortex of the ovary, and causes the typical female growth characteristics. Much larger amounts of oestrogen, produced by the follicle, act on the cow's brain, firstly to inhibit more FSH production and secondly to modify the cow's behaviour and cause her to display oestrus (i.e. to come into season, or displays 'heat'). Oestrogen acts on the reproductive tract at the same time. Blood supply increases and causes the tract to 'tone up'. The vulva swells and becomes distended while the cervix and uterus produce copious quantities of clear stringy mucus.

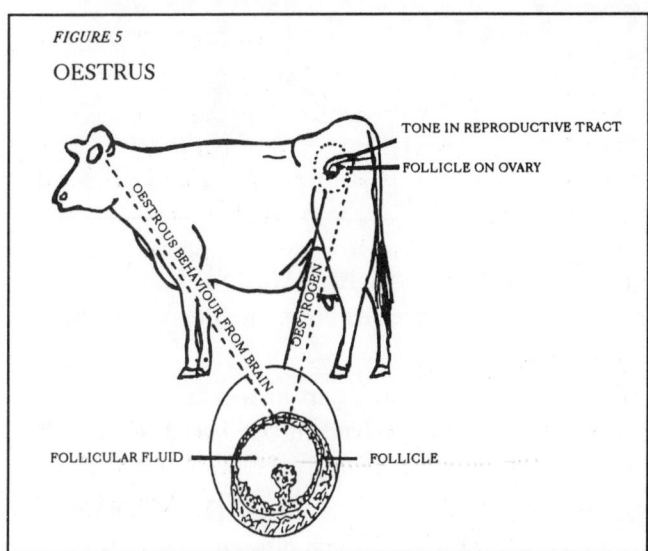

FIGURE 5
OESTRUS

STAGE 3–MET-OESTRUS. Luteinising hormone (LH) is released from the anterior pituitary after oestrus. Peak LH production is reached approximately ten to twelve hours after the end of standing heat. LH causes ovulation (release of the ovum from the follicle) and growth of the corpus luteum at the ovulation site.

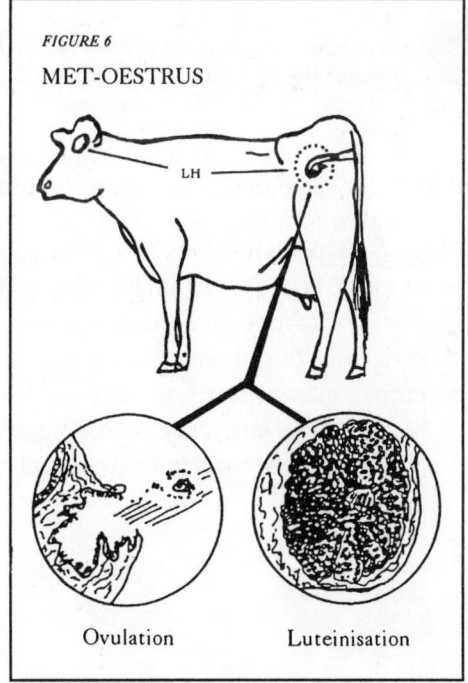

FIGURE 6
MET-OESTRUS

Ovulation   Luteinisation

STAGE 4–DI-OESTRUS. The corpus luteum develops and after three to five days produces progesterone, the pregnancy hormone.

Progesterone acts on the brain, inhibiting LH release and sexual activity.

Progesterone also prepares the reproductive tract for pregnancy and in prolonged concentrations causes udder development. Pregnancy is maintained by progesterone.

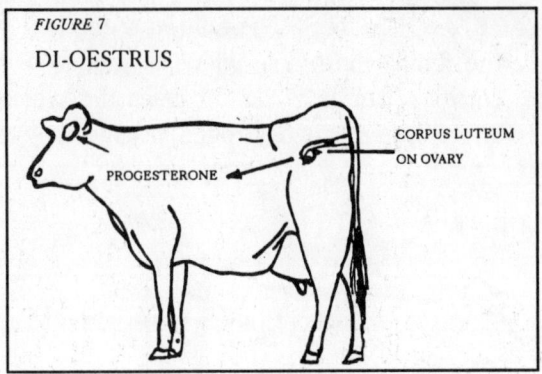

FIGURE 7
DI-OESTRUS

STAGE 5–ALTERNATIVE (A) PRO-OESTRUS (OR STAGE 1 AGAIN). If by Day 19 of the cycle the cow is not pregnant, her uterus releases hormone like compounds called prostaglandins.

(Prostaglandins are present in semen as well, and play a part in sperm transport in the uterus and oviduct. Prostaglandins are also involved in the initial stages of calving.)

Prostaglandins F_2 alpha and E_2 alpha occur naturally in the uterine tissue and their action is to cause luteolysis—dissolving of the corpus luteum. This causes cessation of progesterone production and removes the inhibition to sexual activity, allowing the cycle to start again.

N.B. Administration of synthetic prostaglandins in the first five months of pregnancy (for oestrus synchronisation) may cause abortion due to luteolysis and uterine contraction.

(For the oestrus synchronising action of prostaglandins see the section on oestrus synchronisation in the chapter 'Conducting an Artificial Breeding Program'.)

STAGE 5–ALTERNATIVE (B) ANOESTRUS DUE TO PREGNANCY. The presence of a foetus at Day 19 inhibits the release of prostaglandins from the uterine wall. Because of this the corpus luteum remains and produces progesterone which maintains the pregnancy. At approximately six months into the pregnancy the corpus luteum starts to decline in activity as the cotyledons become the major source of progesterone (see 'Pregnancy and Parturition' below). This transition may lead some cows to show sexual activity (e.g. mounting other cows).

OESTROGEN CAUSES THE COW TO DISPLAY SIGNS OF OESTRUS OR HEAT.

Other Hormones

PROLACTIN. Prolactin, or luteotrophic hormone, is produced in the anterior pituitary gland. Its action is to maintain the corpus luteum and initiate and maintain lactation. It is also involved in maternal behaviour patterns.

OXYTOCIN. Oxytocin, the milk let down hormone, is produced in the posterior pituitary gland. Apart from triggering milk let down, oxytocin also causes contraction of the uterus. This action is involved in sperm transport for fertilisation and also aids in expelling the calf at parturition (birth) and expelling the afterbirth (placenta) immediately after parturition. Gentle massage of the cervix after insemination releases oxytocin and boosts conception chances.

The action of oxytocin is counteracted by the effect of adrenalin which is released when animals get frightened or upset. This reduces chances of conception. Gentle handling and good facilities are essential to prevent upset.

RELAXIN. This is produced by the corpus luteum in very late pregnancy. It causes relaxation of the ligaments around the pelvis, enlarging the birth canal. It is responsible for the characteristics of 'springing' in late pregnancy.

Fertilisation

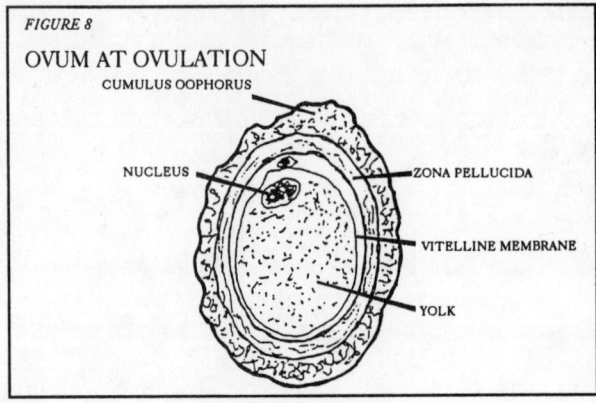

Ovulation is the release of the egg from the ovary. Luteinising hormone gradually softens and breaks down the wall of the follicle so the ovum can mature and float free. When released, the ovum is caught by the infundibulum and passes into the fallopian tube which moves it towards the uterus. Ovulation usually occurs about twelve hours after the end of heat, although its timing varies within a normal range 2 to 26 hours.

Structure of the Ovum

The mature ovum of the cow is similar to other mammalian egg cells.

- The cumulus (or granuloma) cells provide nutrients and protect the ovum.
- The zona pellucida (clear layer) contains two gel layers which protect the ovum. The zona is impervious to most compounds.
- The vitelline membrane covers the yolk.
- The yolk provides nutrients to the rapidly dividing cells of the embryo until they are implanted in the uterus.
- The nucleus contains half of the genetic information which will determine the characteristics of the animals. The other half is from the sperm nucleus.

Ovum Transport

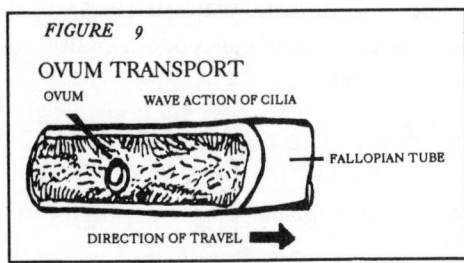

The beating action of the cilia propels the ovum by setting up currents in the fluid secreted by the oviduct. As the egg moves down the tube, excess cumulus cells may be removed by the cilia.

Muscular contractions of the oviduct also contribute to transport of the ovum.

Sperm Transport

In natural mating, semen is deposited in the anterior part of the vagina. Sperm are carried into the uterus by the cervical mucus and some reach the oviduct within two to four minutes. The rapid movement of sperm to the site of fertilisation is believed to be due to contractions of the uterus and oviducts. Oxytocin released at mating stimulates muscular contractions. Prostaglandins in sperm also assist sperm transport in the uterus and oviduct.

Capacitation

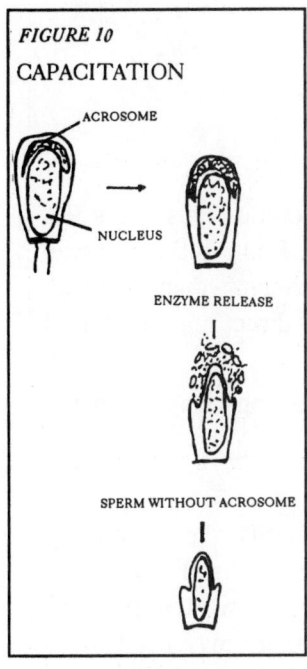

FIGURE 10
CAPACITATION

Sperm must be in the female tract for one to six hours before they are capable of fertilising the egg. During this time they undergo a series of chemical changes which prepare them for penetration and fertilisation of the ovum. This process of change is known as capacitation. It is thought to include the removal of a membrane to expose the enzymes which facilitate penetration of the egg.

Penetration

The enzymes released during capacitation allow sperm to move through the layers of the egg to reach the nucleus. (Enzymes are substances which stimulate chemical reactions. The reactions in this case result in the layers of the egg dissolving to allow the sperm to pass through. Hyaluronidase and trypsin act on cumulus cells and zonalysin acts on the zona pellucida.)

Fertilisation

Fertilisation, by which male and female gametes unite to form the zygote, takes place at a site one-third of the way down the fallopian tube. Sperm are not attracted to the ovum, and fertilisation occurs by a chance collision of the sperm and ovum. The wall of the egg becomes impervious once a spermatozoon has entered, so as to prevent polyspermy, i.e. fertilisation by more than one sperm.

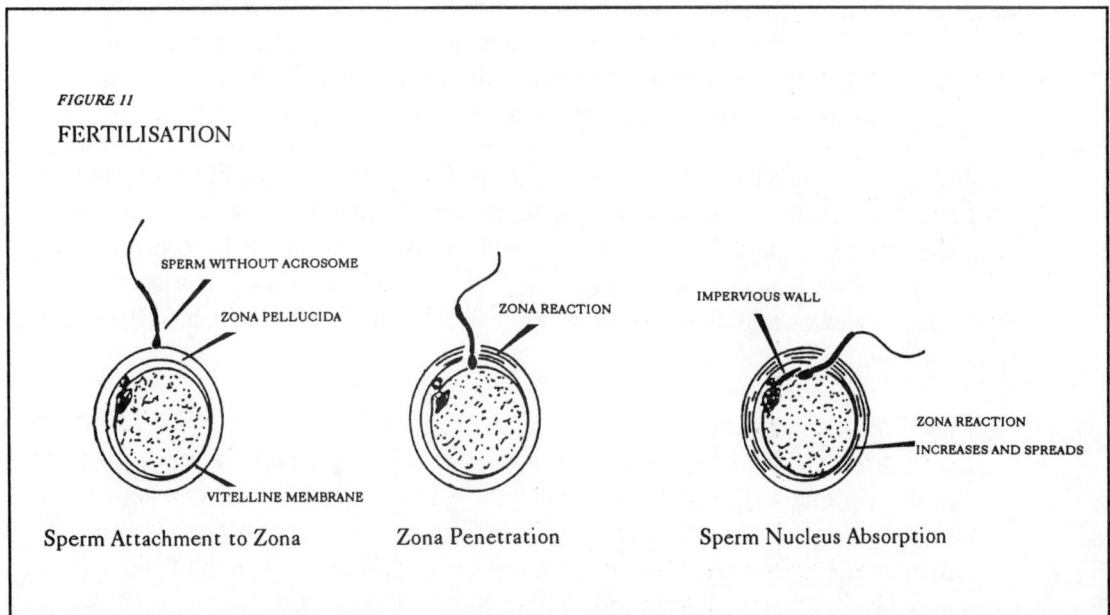

FIGURE 11
FERTILISATION

Zygote: the fertilised egg before it begins to divide.

Gamete: male or female reproductive cell, i.e. sperm or ovum.

Ovum or Embryo Transfer

In nature a cow is limited to ten to fifteen progeny in a lifetime. This limits the direct genetic impact a cow can have on herd improvement. Embryo transfer was developed to enable superior cows to have many more progeny than could be obtained under natural conditions and thus have a far greater direct impact on herd improvement.

Embryo transfers are now offered commercially by veterinarians in many countries.

This process can be divided into five stages.

STAGE 1–INITIAL PREPARATION. The first step is to identify the genetically superior cows by a production recording scheme. The bull to be used should also have his genetic worth assessed by a progeny test or a performance test (refer to the chapter 'Bull Selection'). The suitability of certain matings may need to be assessed by a geneticist.

The genetically superior cow (donor cow) must be empty and cycling normally before the program commences. The cows which are to be used as surrogate mothers (recipient cows) must also be empty and cycling normally.

STAGE 2–TREATMENT OF DONOR COWS. In nature, a cow normally releases only one egg (ovum) at a time for fertilisation. But for an embryo transfer program to be worthwhile the donor cow will need to be treated to ensure the release of numerous ova for fertilisation and transfer to recipient cows. This is done with an injection of FSH, at the correct time in the donor cow's cycle, by a veterinarian. To ensure correct timing, oestrus synchronising drugs such as prostaglandins may be used to control the oestrous cycle of the donor cow.

STAGE 3–TREATMENT OF RECIPIENT COWS. An embryo is most likely to 'take', if the recipient cow is at exactly the same stage of the oestrous cycle as the donor cow. To achieve this, the oestrous cycle of the recipients must be controlled by use of oestrus synchronising drugs such as prostaglandins (see the section on oestrus synchronisation in the chapter 'Conducting an Artificial Breeding Program').

STAGE 4–COLLECTION OF EMBRYOS FROM DONOR COWS. The donor cow is inseminated, sometimes two or three times, during her heat period. Accurate heat detection is critical for good results. Between seven and twelve days later the embryos are removed from the donor cow by nonsurgical means. These embryos are examined microscopically to assess their viability. Up to 30 embryos may be obtained from one collection, but on average only five viable embryos are collected.

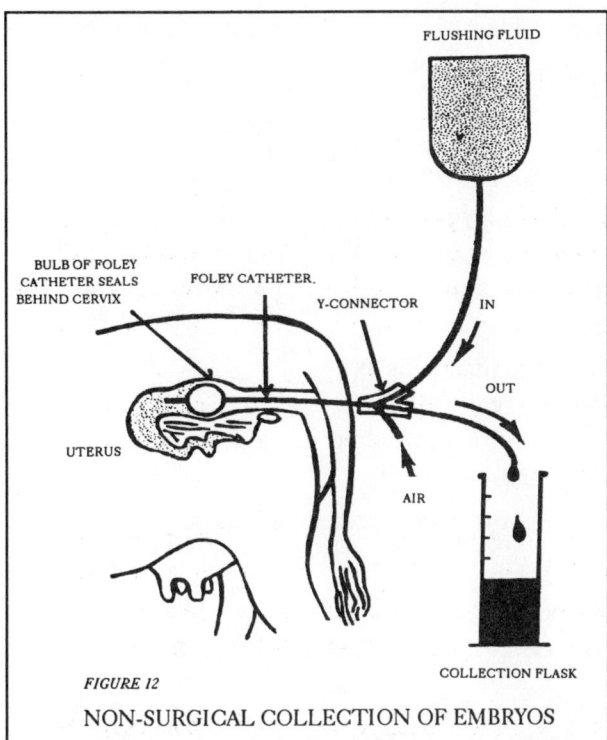

FIGURE 12
NON-SURGICAL COLLECTION OF EMBRYOS

STAGE 5–TRANSFER OF EMBRYOS TO RECIPIENTS. As soon as possible the viable embryos are transferred to the recipient cows. This in the past was usually a surgical procedure but nonsurgical transfers are now done more frequently.

On average up to 60% of all embryos take successfully. The transferred embryo then grows inside the recipient cow just as if it were her own calf.

Pregnancy and Parturition

The duration of pregnancy (the gestation period) in cows is about 283 days, with a normal range of 273 to 291 days. *Bos indicus* and larger European breeds tend to have longer gestations; small breeds such as Jerseys have shorter gestations. Gestation may be divided into two stages:

- The embryonic stage—from fertilisation to Days 45 to 48
- The foetal stage—from Days 45 to 48 to calving.

Within 15 to 30 hours of fertilisation, the zygote divides. At four to five days the embryo has reached the uterus, has 16 to 32 cells, and is termed a morula. At Day 8 the zona pellucida disintegrates and a blastocyst is formed.

On the 14th day the blastocyst attaches loosely to the uterine wall and part of it elongates to form a membrane called the chorion. Uterine 'milk' nourishes the embryo at this stage.

Implantation begins by the 35th day with the chorion and the uterus forming cotyledons or 'buttons'. The embryonic and maternal tissues are closely associated, allowing nutrients to pass from the maternal to the foetal blood supply and waste products to pass in the opposite direction.

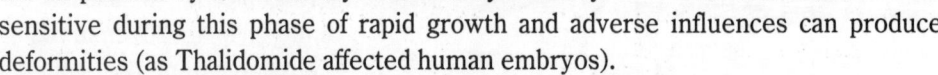

FIGURE 13
COW BLASTOCYST

Cells divide rapidly and the head, heart and limb buds are all present by the 40th day. The embryo is very sensitive during this phase of rapid growth and adverse influences can produce deformities (as Thalidomide affected human embryos).

Organs continue to differentiate during the foetal stage, and there is a rapid increase in weight, particularly in the last 60 days, when the foetus trebles in size.

Pregnancy Diagnosis

HORMONAL ASSAY. Changes in hormone levels in samples of blood or urine are used to diagnose pregnancy in humans and horses. Hormone levels in milk may be used to detect pregnancy in cows if the milk sample is taken at an accurate, specified time after mating. Hormone assays are expensive and not yet practical for commercial use.

BEHAVIOUR. Changes in behaviour due to hormone balance will allow some observers to detect animals which are in calf. Absence of oestrus activity is the most reliable behavioural guide, but the accuracy of pregnancy diagnosis by this method is low.

SONAR. Sonar machines are being used to detect pregnancy in a number of species including cattle. Changes to the wavelength of a reflected soundwave (the doppler effect) can be interpreted to indicate whether or not the animal is pregnant. This method is not entirely satisfactory in cattle as diagnosis of empty (non-pregnant) cows is difficult.

REAL TIME ULTRASONOGRAPHY. This method employs the doppler effect as do sonar pregnancy testing machines. Here the reflected soundwaves are converted into visual images on a screen instead of audible sound. Considerable skill is needed to interpret these images for an accurate diagnosis.

HISTOLOGY. Pregnancy can be detected by examining the cells and mucus of the cervix and vagina under a microscope. This method is reliable but not practical for commercial use.

PALPATION. Diagnosis of pregnancy by palpation of the tract per rectum (PR)—i.e. by feeling through the cow's rectal passage—is the most effective method. The technique is classed as an act of veterinary surgery in many places and only veterinarians are permitted to offer the service, but owners of stock are permitted to diagnose pregnancy in their own cattle in most situations.

Per Rectum Pregnancy Diagnosis

As with all *per rectum* examinations it is advisable to get the cow as relaxed as possible. The excessive moving and straining of nervous cattle lead to inaccurate diagnosis. Straining due to molasses and rye grass feeding also reduces accuracy.

1. DAYS 28 TO 35. Detection of very early pregnancy requires skill and is not advisable because of the risk of causing abortion. Great care must be exercised if the procedure is attempted. Gentle palpation reveals:

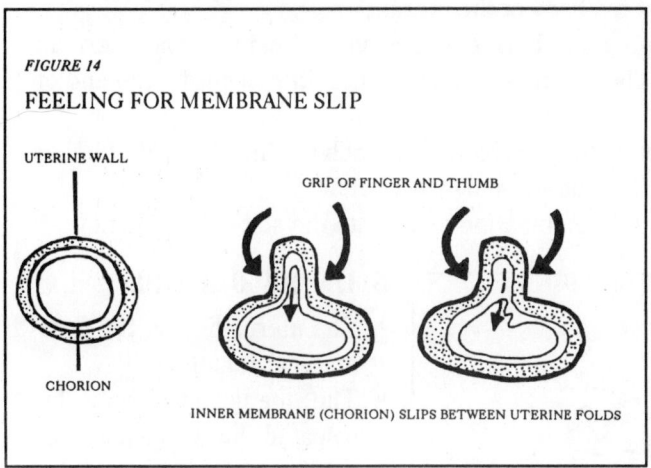

FIGURE 14
FEELING FOR MEMBRANE SLIP

- the corpus luteum on the ovary of the pregnant uterine horn
- an abrupt end to the pregnant uterine horn
- membrane slip, detectable after the 30th day. By grasping the uterus gently with the thumb and finger, the chorion can be felt slipping between the folded uterine walls. The best site to feel this is where the horns curl around.

This technique should be attempted only by veterinarians or very experienced operators as it is possible to damage the membranes and developing embryo and cause abortion.

2. DAYS 35 TO 62. At this stage, examination should still only be attempted by a veterinarian or very experienced operator because of the risk of damage to the membranes and the embryo, and of abortion.

- The pregnant horn tends to straighten out, i.e. to lose its curl. It has a fluid tone and an increased diameter when compared to the non-pregnant horn.
- The extra weight of the pregnant horn often twists the tract slightly, leaving the lighter, more tightly curled, non-pregnant horn 'floating' on top.

3. DAYS 62 TO 90. Experienced operators should be able to detect pregnancy by 63 days.

- The uterus feels like a water filled rubber balloon with a diameter of 10-16 cm.

- The horns are no longer symmetrical and the difference in size becomes gradually more apparent towards the 90th day.
- Very gentle palpation of the uterus will reveal a foetus the size of a mouse at 60 days and the size of a rat at 90 days.
- The uterus should still be in the pelvic cavity or in the upper part of the abdominal cavity.

4. **DAYS 90 TO 150.** Pregnancy testing after 90 days should be a relatively risk free proposition to most trained operators.
    - The uterus descends into the abdominal cavity and becomes progressively more difficult to palpate.
    - Its size increases mainly due to the volume of fluid in the membranes.
    - The foetus weighs about 2 to 3 kg and is about the size of a cat at 150 days.
    - Cotyledons can be detected. At 90 days they have a diameter of about 1 to 2 cm (like a 5 cent coin); at 150 days, 3 cm (like a 20 cent coin). The size of the cotyledons is best gauged at the body of the uterus.
    - The uterine artery of the pregnant horn enlarges and develops a characteristic 'buzzing pulse' (fremitus). The artery is as thick as the little finger by the end of gestation.
    - The weight of the uterus pulls the cervix over the pelvic brim. Instead of being hard and muscular, the cervix enlarges and feels doughy.

    These signs must be identified in combination to indicate the state of pregnancy.

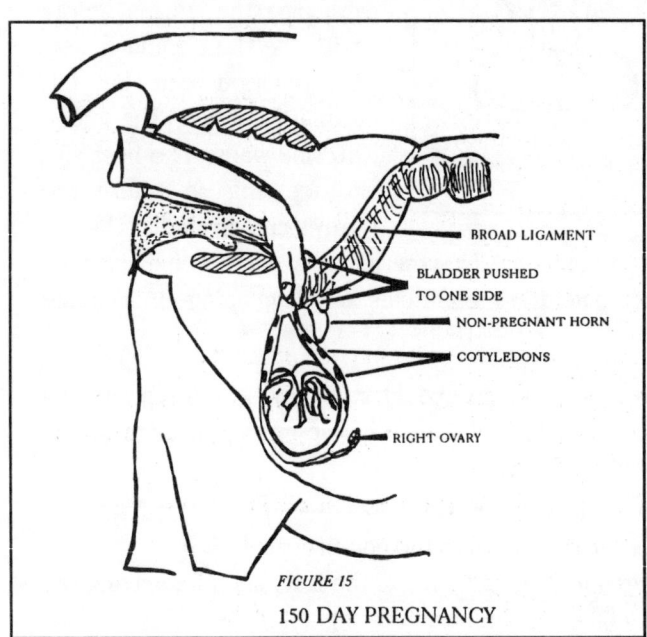

FIGURE 15
150 DAY PREGNANCY

5. **DAYS 150 TO 210.**
    - The uterus lies on the floor of the abdomen.
    - The foetus may only be palpated by bouncing, i.e. gentle pressure on the uterine fluid so as to bounce the foetus against the hand.
    - Cotyledons and fremitus are readily detectable.
    - The foetus is the size of a small dog (9 to 13 kg).

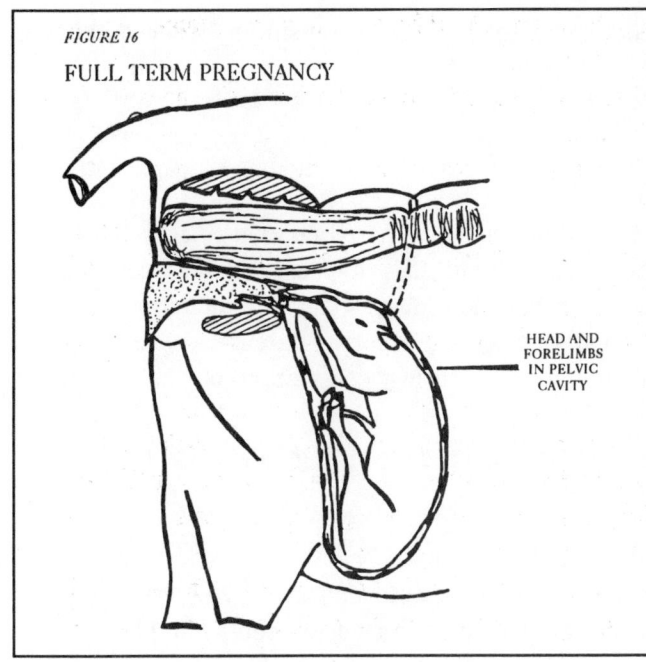

FIGURE 16
FULL TERM PREGNANCY

HEAD AND FORELIMBS IN PELVIC CAVITY

6. DAY 210 TO CALVING.

- The foetus enlarges and is easy to feel.
- Palpation of the foetus may elicit movement.
- Close to calving the foetus should lie with its forelimbs extended towards the pelvic outlet and its head between the legs. The head and its features, jaws and ears etc., are easily delineated. The foetus may have one or two teeth at 270 days and may 'bite' at a hand palpating around its jaw.

External Signs of Pregnancy

In heifers the udder increases in size at four to five months and this is a sign of pregnancy. It is not normally evident in mature cows until one to four weeks before calving.

From six months onward (later in fat cows), foetal movements may be seen through the abdominal wall. In some cows the foetal heart sounds may be heard from the seventh month with the aid of a stethoscope.

Abdominal swelling is not usually noticeable until the later stages of pregnancy.

Signs of Approaching Parturition

Some signs are observable in cows and heifers, others in one or other.

- In cows, the udder enlarges one to four weeks before calving. This is not a reliable sign in heifers as the udder begins to develop halfway through pregnancy.
- Production of colostrum—a creamy or pink secretion—begins from the udder.
- The white stringy vaginal mucus becomes more profuse.
- The mucus plug in the cervix liquefies.
- The animal usually moves to a quiet spot away from the rest of the herd.
- Heifers may become restless and lose their appetite.
- Pelvic ligaments relax under the influence of relaxin, 24 to 48 hours before

calving, making the tail appear to be set higher and causing a looser walking action, i.e. 'springing'.
- The vulva swells to six times its normal size.

Induction of Parturition

Birth is brought on by the foetus producing a hormone which acts on the cotyledons and uterus to release prostaglandins. It is the foetus which determines when birth commences, not the mother. (The timing is partly hereditary—see p. 77.) Prostaglandins (mainly F_2 alpha) dissolve the corpus luteum, consequently lowering the levels of progesterone and causing contraction of the uterine muscles.

Oxytocin is released in the later stages to increase the strength of contractions.

Stages of Parturition

The calf is normally presented with the forelimbs extended and its head resting on, or between them. In some instances the hind limbs may be presented first.

STAGE 1. The uterine muscles contract to force the foetal membranes through the dilating cervix. Contractions gradually increase in frequency as the second stage approaches.

STAGE 2. The foetal membranes (water bag) and feet approach the vulva. Abdominal contractions, which are under voluntary control, take over the main effort of expelling the foetus. The cow may rest for a short time after the head is presented before resuming contractions to push the foetus out of the birth canal. This stage takes between 30 minutes and four hours to complete.

STAGE 3. The foetal membranes are normally expelled within eight hours. If they are still in place after 24 hours, veterinary attention should be sought.

Difficult Calving (dystocia)

Any calving in which the second stage takes longer than four hours should be viewed with concern. If dystocia occurs veterinary attention should be sought. Intervention by an untrained person will usually aggravate the situation. Dystocia can be reduced by careful management. It is advisable to keep calving cows (particularly heifers) under observation.

Lactation (period of suckling)

Oestrogen promotes growth of the duct system of the udder while progesterone stimulates development of the milk secreting glands (alveoli).

Prolactin has a dual role. Before calving it stimulates udder development; after calving it encourages milk production. It is thought that high levels of progesterone during pregnancy suppress the milk forming action. This suppression stops when progesterone levels fall at calving.

Colostrum (first milk) is a rich source of antibodies which prevent infection until the calf builds up its own resistance (immunity).

SUCKLING CAUSES RELEASE OF OXYTOCIN.

Suckling stimulates the release of oxytocin (milk let down hormone) to cause contraction of the milk secreting tissues. Milk is forced into the ducts and teats to facilitate easy removal.

ANATOMY AND PHYSIOLOGY OF THE BULL

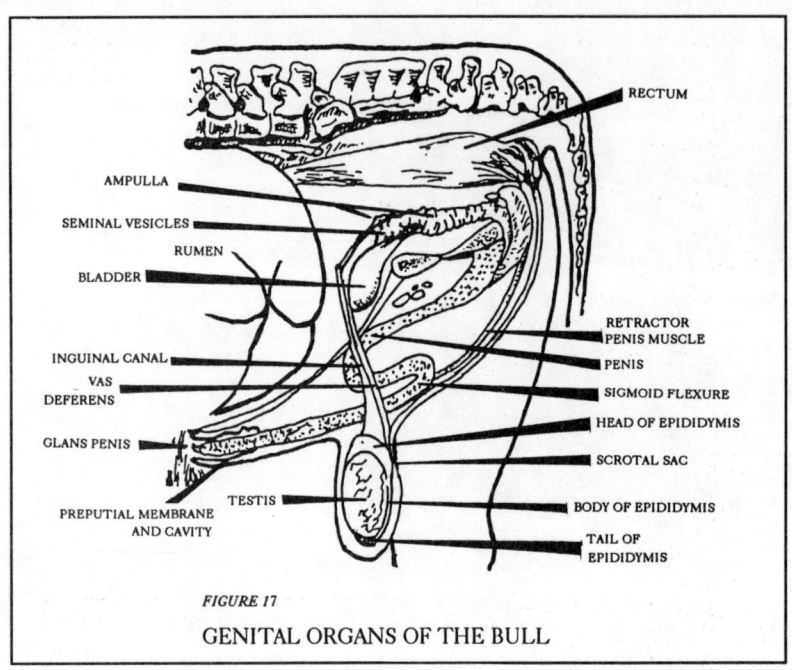

FIGURE 17
GENITAL ORGANS OF THE BULL

Testicles (Testes)

The testicles are paired organs found in a sac like structure (the scrotum). The surface of the testes is covered by the tunica albuginea, a closely adhering thin white fibrous sheath. When it is cut, the soft testicular tissue bulges through.

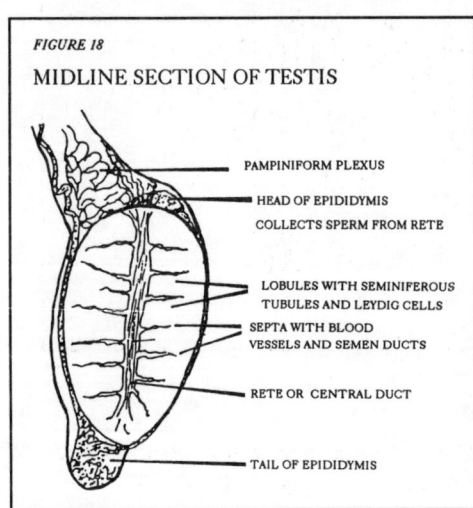

FIGURE 18
MIDLINE SECTION OF TESTIS

The testicles of a mature bull perform two functions:
- spermatogenesis: production of spermatozoa
- production of the male sex hormone, testosterone.

Spermatozoa are single living cells which constitute the basic unit of reproduction in the male. They are formed in the seminiferous tubules of the testes under the control of FSH and LH. Each testicle contains about 2000 m of seminiferous tubule producing 20,000 sperm per second. Spermatogenesis takes 60 days to complete.

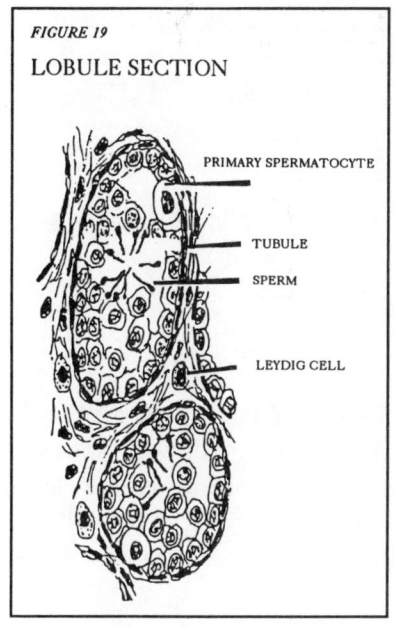

FIGURE 19
LOBULE SECTION

Leydig cells, located between the loops of seminiferous tubule, produce testosterone, which has two major functions:

- it induces libido (sex drive)
- it causes development of male characteristics in the bull's neck region. These include muscular development, heavier forequarters and the crest.

Scrotum

The scrotum is a two lobed sac, the lobes being divided by a vertical septum. It is composed of a number of layers:

- the skin, which should be almost hairless or have only very fine hairs
- the tunica dartos muscle
- the tunica vaginalis, a thick white fibrous sheath surround-ing the testes. The dorsal part is attached to the cremaster muscle which enables the bull to draw the testes towards the abdomen.

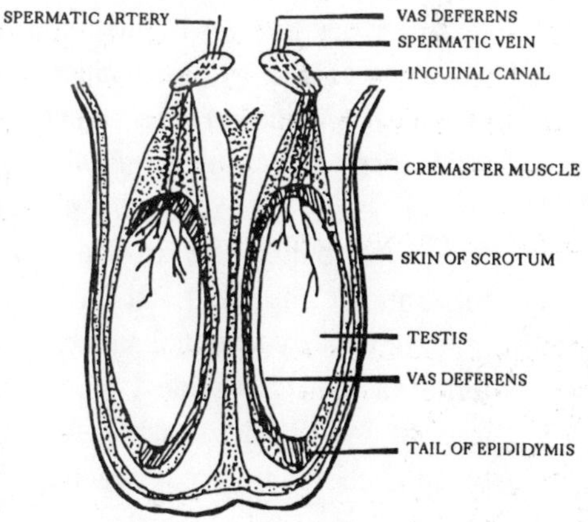

The scrotum has three main functions:

- to support the testes
- to protect the testes
- to regulate temperature within the testes.

FIGURE 20
VERTICAL SECTION OF SCROTUM AND TESTES

TEMPERATURE REGULATION IN THE TESTES. The optimum temperature for spermatogenesis is 33° to 36°C (3° to 6° *below* body temperature). Variation above or below this range impairs sperm production. Heat stress increases the numbers of abnormal sperm in an ejaculate. In the epididymis such abnormalities show up as returned tails, retained droplets and increased mortality. Sperm in the seminiferous tubules show the damage as abnormal heads, midpieces and tails.

Temperature of the testes is controlled by:

- Evaporation of sweat
  The skin of the scrotum is well supplied with sweat glands. Heat from the body of the testes is conducted by the blood to the skin, which is cooled by evaporating sweat. The efficiency of this cooling depends on the temperature, humidity and movement of air in immediate contact with the scrotum.

- Muscle contraction
  The muscular tunica dartos and the cremaster muscle contract in cold weather and relax in hot weather. In this way the testes and scrotum are drawn towards the warm body wall to conserve heat in cold weather and are lowered away from the body in warm weather. Lowering also increases the surface area of the scrotum to expose more skin for sweat evaporation. *Bos indicus* animals display this quite markedly.

- Blood supply
  Blood coming to the testes via the spermatic artery is at body temperature (39°C). If it went straight into the testes it would raise the temperature and disrupt spermatogenesis. Venous blood leaving the testes is cooler (33°C) because of its close association with the scrotum which is cooled by the evaporation of sweat. Veins in the spermatic cord form a complex network of vessels (the pampiniform plexus) which surrounds the arteries. Due to transfer of heat, there is a tendency to equalisation of temperature between blood in arterial and venous vessels. Arterial blood is cooled before it reaches the testes.

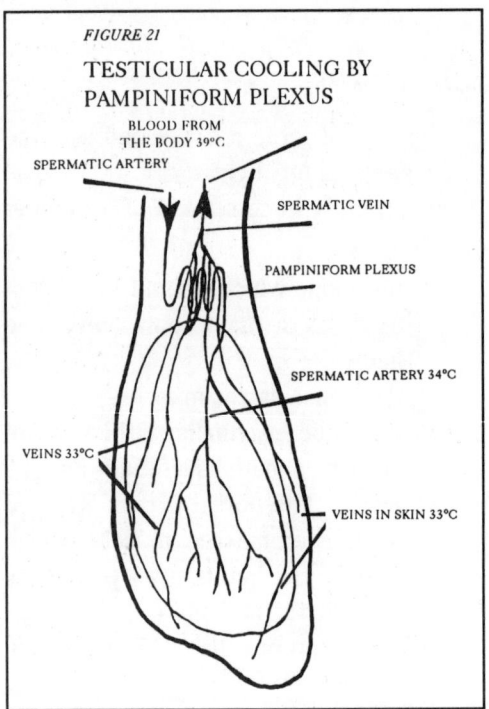

FIGURE 21

TESTICULAR COOLING BY PAMPINIFORM PLEXUS

BLOOD FROM THE BODY 39°C
SPERMATIC ARTERY
SPERMATIC VEIN
PAMPINIFORM PLEXUS
SPERMATIC ARTERY 34°C
VEINS 33°C
VEINS IN SKIN 33°C

Epididymis

The epididymis is divided into three parts:

- the head is on the top part of the testicle and is very closely attached to it
- the body extends down the outside of the testicle
- the tail is the enlarged distal part which may be palpated at the base of the testicle.

The epididymis has a number of functions including:

- sperm storage
- provision of nutrients for sperm
- maturation of sperm as they move down the epididymis. Immature sperm are incapable of fertilisation.

Vas Deferens

The vas deferens connects the epididymis to the urethra. It is a thin whitish tube which enters the body through the inguinal canal and terminates at the ampulla. The vas deferens contracts during ejaculation to force sperm down the urethra.

Ampulla

The ampulla is a thickened glandular extension of the vas deferens. It acts as a valve to prevent urination while the bull is sexually excited. It also stops urine from entering the vas deferens.

Urethra

The urethra runs the length of the penis and is the common duct for both urine and sperm.

Accessory Glands

The seminal vesicles, prostate, and bulbo-urethral glands make up the accessory sex glands. Their function is to produce seminal plasma (accessory fluid) which may form 60% to 95% of the volume of an ejaculate. Seminal plasma has a number of functions:

- It cleanses the urethra of urine, bacteria and contaminants just before ejaculation. This is seen when the bull 'dribbles' a bit just before mounting.
- It activates sperm.
- It provides nutrients for the sperm.
- It adds volume to the ejaculate.
- It may aid sperm survival in the vagina. The vagina is a hostile environment for sperm and unless they can quickly gain entry to the uterus, they will die. Seminal plasma may prolong sperm survival in the vagina until more sperm can gain entry to the uterus.

The Penis

The bull's penis is fibro-elastic material covered by a dense white fibrous sheet—the tunica albuginea. There is some erectile tissue present but this is minimal when compared to that found in horses and humans. In a bull the erectile tissue is only for hardening the penis during erection and not for lengthening it or increasing the diameter. Erection is caused by contraction of muscles at the root of the penis.

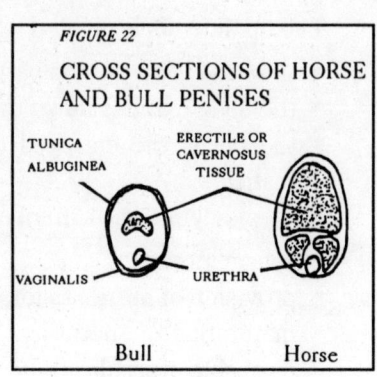

FIGURE 22
CROSS SECTIONS OF HORSE AND BULL PENISES

The end of the penis (the glans penis) is about 8cm long. It is flattened and slightly twisted. At ejaculation, the glans twists about half to one turn to increase the effective diameter of the penis.

Prepuce

The prepuce, or sheath, is the protective covering of the penis.

SEMEN—COLLECTION, PROCESSING AND STORAGE

AB Centre Operations

Most AB centres use an artificial vagina to collect semen. With this device, temperature, pressure and friction are used to stimulate ejaculation when the donor bull mounts a teaser animal. Cows may be used as teasers but have disadvantages. Other bulls or steers are satisfactory. In some instances mechanical decoys are used.

Demand for a bull's semen determines the frequency of collection. Two ejaculates twice a week (e.g. two on Monday and two on Thursday), will allow an average bull to produce 30,000 doses or more in a year.

When bulls are unable to mount because of injury or some other factor, electro-ejaculation can be used. This method employs passage of a fluctuating current between electrodes on a probe which is placed in the bull's rectum. This current stimulates accessory sex glands and the muscles of ejaculation. Electro-ejaculation is usually regarded as a *last resort* for semen collection. It is time consuming, requires expensive equipment and risks injury to the donor animal. Semen quality is not as good as that collected by the artificial vagina.

Processing

About ten million normal, actively moving sperm are required to produce conception using artificial insemination. They must be placed at the correct site in the reproductive tract of a cow which is at the correct stage of the breeding cycle.

When processing a dose of frozen semen, the aim is to ensure that sufficient live sperm are present for conception when the dose is thawed to body temperature.

Processing includes: evaluation, dilution, cooling, packing, freezing, quality control (evaluation after freezing) and storage.

1. **EVALUATION.** After examining a drop of raw semen under low power on a microscope to obtain an estimate of sperm concentration and activity, samples are taken for detailed assessment. One drop is placed in a test tube with a special stain to determine the percentage of the spermatozoa which were alive and of normal conformation at the time of staining.

    Another drop is used to ascertain the density of the raw semen—the number of sperm per millilitre. A spectrophotometer measures the amount of light passing through the sample of semen diluted at a particular rate. By multiplying the volume of the ejaculate by the density and the percentage of live sperm, the total number of live sperm in the ejaculate can be worked out.

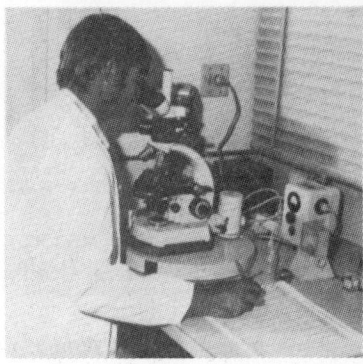
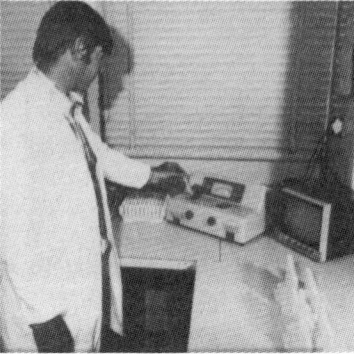

LEFT: LOW MAGNIFICATION INITIAL ASSESSMENT OF SEMEN QUALITY.

RIGHT: ESTIMATION OF DENSITY BY SPECTROPHOTOMETER.

2. **DILUTION (OR EXTENSION).** An average ejaculate may contain 5000 million sperm in 5 ml of raw semen. Super-fertile mature bulls may yield up to 12,000 million sperm per ejaculate.

With natural service this could only produce one calf. By diluting the ejaculate, the raw semen can be extended to give 200 or more individual 0·25 ml doses each containing 25 million live sperm. While only 10 million sperm are required for conception, more than double this number are placed in the straw to allow for losses during freezing. Glycerol is the chemical added to prevent death of sperm during the freezing process. Diluents may be based on skim milk, egg yolk citrate or specially prepared chemical diluents such as TRIS with egg yolk. Antibiotics are added as a precautionary measure and most diluents have added fructose (fruit sugar) to supply energy to the sperm.

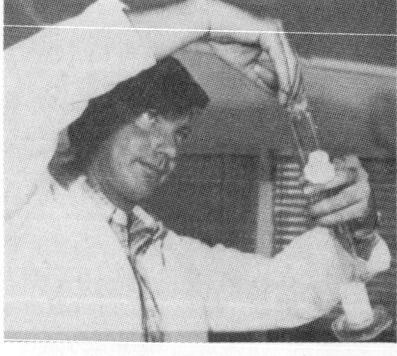
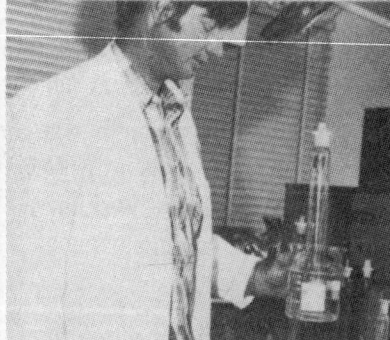

LEFT: DILUTION OF RAW SEMEN

RIGHT: DILUTED SEMEN IN WATER BATH FOR CONTROLLED COOLING.

3. **PACKING.** More than 200 AB centres around the world use the Cassou or French straw system for packing semen. Glass ampoules were used originally but in most countries, these have been replaced by straws.

The medium straw (0·5 ml volume) was introduced in 1965 and the 'mini-straw' (0·25 ml volume) in 1969.

Cassou straws are 133 mm long poly-vinyl chloride tubes. Medium straws have a 3 mm diameter and mini-straws 2 mm. They are plugged at one end (the double plug end) with a sealing powder which is retained between two cotton plugs. By applying a vacuum to this end of the straw, semen can be drawn up the tube and into contact with the sealing powder. As soon as the powder becomes wet it turns into a gel to provide a very effective seal. Automatic straw filling and sealing machines use an ultrasonic pulse to seal the other end (the laboratory end).

4. **COOLING AND FREEZING.** At body temperature sperm swim about very rapidly, exhaust their energy reserves in a relatively short time, and die.

The rate of a chemical reaction depends on the temperature at which the process is taking place. If the temperature is reduced, the rate of reaction is also reduced. Cooling semen to near freezing point slows the sperm down, by slowing their internal reactions, and extends their life for several days if they are protected by suitable chemicals. By further cooling, activity can be effectively stopped to give

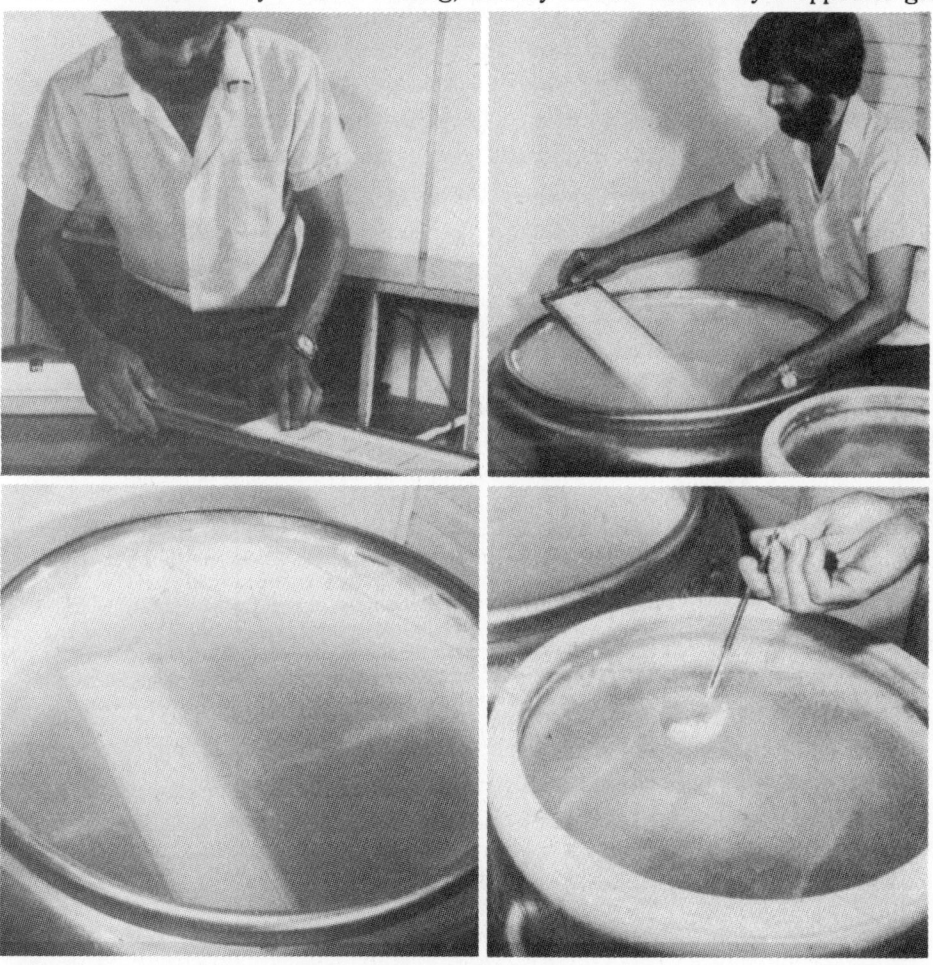

ABOVE LEFT: STRAWS ARE LOADED ON A RACK. ABOVE RIGHT: THE LOADED RACK IS LOWERED IN LIQUID NITROGEN VAPOUR. BELOW LEFT: STRAWS ARE PLACED IN VAPOUR FOR FREEZING. BELOW RIGHT: FREEZING IS COMPLETED IN LIQUID NITROGEN.

the sperm an almost indefinite life. Some of the sperm are killed in the freezing process but with correct processing, many survive and will revive on thawing.

The temperature at which semen must be held if it is to retain the ability to fertilise is below minus 80°C. (i.e. 80°C below the freezing point of water.) This is much colder than the temperatures maintained in domestic deep freeze refrigerators. Liquid nitrogen boils at a temperature of minus 196°C. (196°C below the freezing point of water), so it is the most suitable refrigerant available. Straws of semen are frozen by suspending them in the vapour above the surface of the liquid nitrogen, to give a controlled rate of cooling and freezing. They are then stored in the liquid nitrogen until use.

5. **QUALITY CONTROL.** Twenty four hours after freezing, a portion of each batch of semen is thawed and examined under a microscope. If the batch meets prescribed minimum standards for survival and motility, it is packed into goblets and transferred to storage units. Periodically, straws from each batch are checked for signs of deterioration in storage.

6. **STORAGE.** For ease of handling and to minimise the risk of damage to the sperm through exposure, straws are always packed in plastic goblets. Semen should only be transferred to and from liquid nitrogen containers in goblets, because there is **no safe exposure** time for individual straws.

Goblets are usually marked with the bull's common name (the secondary identifier) and the batch number (see below).

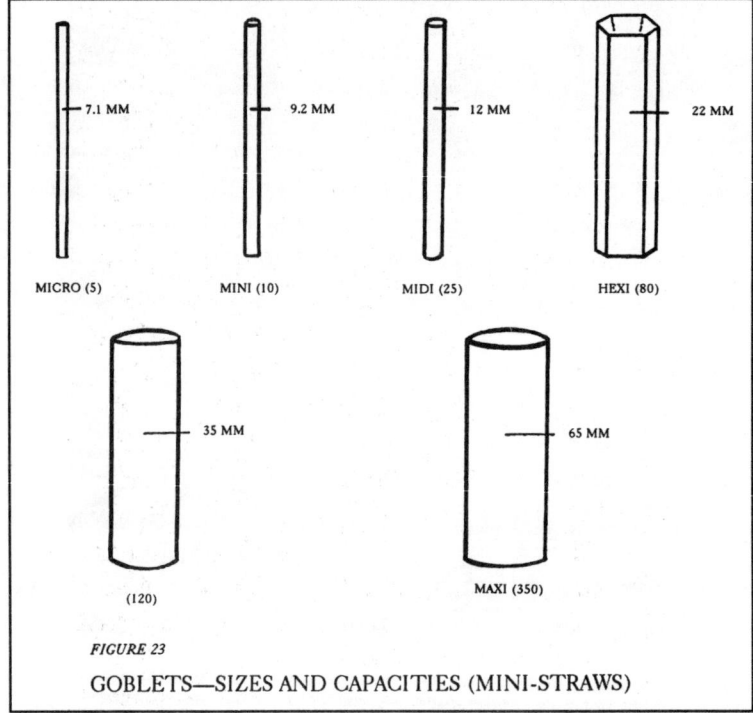

FIGURE 23

GOBLETS—SIZES AND CAPACITIES (MINI-STRAWS)

AB CENTRE OPERATIONS * 35

Identification of Straws

Identification of individual straws in storage is not easy but following the guidelines below will assist.

SEMEN LOCATION. All suitable on farm liquid nitrogen containers have numbered slots for seating each of the buckets. (Refer to the section on liquid nitrogen containers, below.) A 'semen map' on the lid of the liquid nitrogen container or in the kit box is a useful guide for locating semen stocks.

STRAW COLOUR OR TIP COLOUR. Where possible most reputable AB centres will place the different breeds of bulls in the appropriate coloured straws or in clear straws with the tip coloured the appropriate colour. This can help to identify the breed, and hence often the individual bull, at a glance.

Breed colours and tip colours which should be used by major Australian centres (and many overseas centres) are:

	CODE LETTERS	TIP COLOUR (if different to straw colour)	STRAW COLOUR
Africander	AF	-	Red
AFS	FS	-	Red
AMZ	MZ	-	Red
Angus	AA	-	Orange
Aussie Red	UU	Red	Clear
Ayrshire	AY	-	Dark Blue
Bazadaise	BZ	-	Clear
Belgian Blue	BL	-	Clear
Belmont Red	BR	-	Red
Blonde d'Aquitane	BA	Green	Clear
Boran	BN	-	Clear
Braford	BF	Green	Clear
Brahman	BB	Black	Clear
Brahmousin	BX	-	Clear
Braler	BX	-	Clear
Brangus	BG	Pink	Clear
Braunvieh	BV	-	Clear
Charbray	CB	Orange	Clear
Charolais	CC	-	Purple
Chianina	CI	-	Black
Dairy Shorthorn	DS	Red	Pink
Danish Red	DR	Black	Turquoise
Devon	DD	Red	Clear
Dexter	DX	-	Clear

[handwritten note next to "Red" entries at top: "dosent stand"]

	CODE LETTERS	TIP COLOUR	STRAW COLOUR
Droughtmaster	DM	Yellow	Clear
Friesian (Holstein)	FF	-	Grey
Gelbvieh	GB	Clear	Clear
Guernsey	GG	-	Yellow
Hereford	HH	Brown	Clear
Illawarra	IS	-	Turquoise
Jersey	JJ	-	Green
Limousin	LL	Yellow	Clear or Black
Low Line	LA	-	Orange
Maine Anjou	MU	Black	Clear
Murray Grey	MG	-	Salmon
Norwegian Red	UU	Black	Turquoise
Piedmontese	PT	-	Clear
Pinzgauer	PG	-	Clear
Poll Shorthorn	SP	Blue	Red
Poll Hereford	PH	Blue	Clear or Brown
Red Poll	RP	Yellow	Clear
Red Angus	RA	Red	Orange
Romagnola	RO	Black	Clear
Sahiwal	SW	Green	Red
Saler	SL	Green	Clear
Santa Gertrudis	SG	Red	Clear or Bright Red
Shorthorn	BS	-	Red
Simbrah	SM	-	Clear
Simmental	SI	-	Clear
South Devon	SD	Green	Clear
Swedish Red & White	SR	Black	Turquoise
Tarentaise	TA	-	Clear
Texas Longhorn	LH	-	Clear
Tuli	TU	-	Clear
Wagyu	W	-	Clear

GOBLET MARKING. Any goblet purchased from a reputable AB centre will contain semen from one bull only. Two or more bulls' straws should *never* be put in the same goblet.

Goblets may be of different colours and this may assist in identifying straws of a particular bull.

Most reputable AB centres also mark each goblet with a bull's secondary identifier and batch number. (Refer to NASIS codes below.)

Remember, there is *no safe exposure time for an individual straw*. However, a goblet may safely be lifted free of the bucket of a liquid nitrogen container for a short time—sufficient to read the goblet markings.

STRAW MARKING (NASIS CODES). NASIS stands for the National AB Sire Identification Scheme. The objective of NASIS is to give each licensed Artificial Breeders sire a national and unique code to identify a bull and his progeny for genetic assessment schemes such as those conducted by the Australian Dairy Herd Improvement Scheme and by the ABRI for the beef industry (see the chapter 'Bull Selection').

Each straw of semen from reputable AB centres carries in full or in code the following information:
- the centre of origin
- the bull's full name
- the primary and secondary identifiers
- the batch number.

CENTRE OF ORIGIN. The name of the AB centre will be printed on the straw and/or will be part of the NASIS code. (For example, straws collected at the QDPI AB Centre will have WACOL or BILOELA printed on the them.)

The centre codes most commonly seen in Australia are:

CODE	ORGANISATION	LOCATION OF AB CENTRE
11	Genetics Australia	Bacchus Marsh
15	Beef Breeding Services	Wacol
	(Qld Dept of Primary Industries)	Biloela
21	BOSEM	Bundanoon
	(Bovine Semen Aust. Pty Ltd)	
29	R.AB (Riverina Artificial Breeders)	Albury
35	New Zealand Dairy Board	Hamilton, NZ
45	England	Various
70	Canada	Various

BULL'S FULL NAME. The full name of the bull and sometimes his herd book number are printed on the straw.

PRIMARY AND SECONDARY IDENTIFIERS (NASIS CODE). As an example, the bull RIMFIRE KIERAN K14 has the NASIS code:

15	AA	K	01	WPRIMKE
(i)	(ii)	(iii)	(iv)	(v)

(i)   15—the QDPI code number
(ii) AA—breed code for Aberdeen Angus
(iii) K—year of birth, i.e. 1990
(iv) 01—bull number
(v)   WPRIMKE—secondary identifier

So Rimfire Kieran K14 was the first Aberdeen Angus bull born in 1990 to enter a QDPI AB Collection Centre. The year letter sequence is as follows:

K – 1990
L – 1991
M – 1992
N – 1993
P – 1994
R – 1995
S – 1996

Letters I, O and Q are not used in the NASIS year code sequence. Many breed societies use the 'year letters' as initials in the bulls' names. Rimfire Kieran is an example.

BATCH NUMBER. Batch numbers specify the year and day of collection for each straw of semen (e.g. 94135 means a collection on the 135th day of 1994). Records of each day's collections and the number of straws processed are kept by the centre of origin.

Unlicensed Semen

Unlicensed semen is intended for use only by the owner or part owners of a particular bull. It is an excellent form of insurance for valuable bulls.

Generally bulls collected for unlicensed semen production have only undergone minimal health testing. The semen is also often processed on non-licensed premises and may not meet the standards of quality control expected by purchasers of semen.

Unlicensed semen is generally processed into wine red straws which should be identified by the letters UL. Other information, usually in code, includes:

- the owner's name
- the collector/processor/AB centre
- the bull's name
- the breed
- the date of collection.

Liquid Nitrogen Containers

All frozen semen used in Australia is transported and stored under liquid nitrogen, which is by far the most satisfactory refrigerant in terms of operator safety, ease of handling and availability. It also has a wide margin of safety in the temperature range for storage.

Eighty per cent of the air we breathe is nitrogen gas. It can be converted to a liquid by cooling and compressing. The liquid has a boiling point of minus 196°C. Both the liquid and gaseous forms are relatively inert chemically and will not burn, support combustion or react in any way with other materials. These properties make it a very suitable refrigerant.

SAFETY PRECAUTIONS. Liquid nitrogen can be dangerous if not handled correctly because of its extremely low temperature. The following points must be given strict attention.

Avoid contact with the liquid. Prolonged contact with the skin or contact with wet skin may result in severe burns. Contact with eyes (which are continually moistened by tears) may severely affect eyesight.

Use metal forceps when removing straws from liquid nitrogen containers. Skin, if in contact with the cold metal of the buckets, will often stick and tear when removed.

Insert objects into the liquid very slowly. This avoids the splashing which occurs when the liquid boils on insertion of 'warm' objects.

When refilling containers pour the liquid slowly. This avoids 'blow out'. If the nitrogen boils vigorously it may shoot out the neck of the container.

Provide adequate ventilation when storing or transporting. Nitrogen gas is colourless, odourless and tasteless and, although inert, may cause dizziness and suffocation at very high concentrations because of the exclusion of normal air.

When transporting, always place a seat belt around the container or secure it in a safe position. This prevents the container falling over and spilling the liquid. The intense cold of liquid nitrogen will crack all upholstery on contact and may also fill the cabin of the car with a mist from condensed water vapour in the air. The mist may impair vision and cause a serious accident.

Use only the stopper supplied with the container. The stopper is designed to allow controlled evaporation of the liquid nitrogen. Attempted use of other stoppers will lead to dangerous pressure build up or to excessive loss of nitrogen.

FIRST AID. Flood the affected area with large quantities of unheated water and later apply cold compresses. If the skin is blistered, or if eyes or other delicate tissues are affected, seek medical attention immediately.

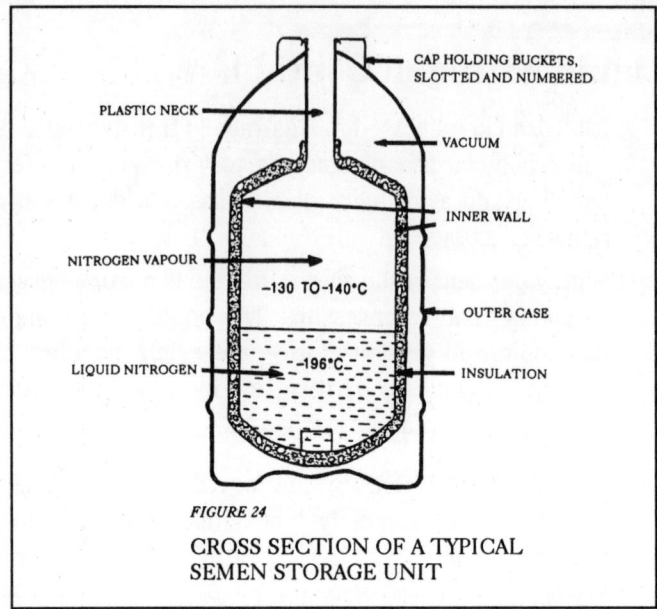

FIGURE 24

CROSS SECTION OF A TYPICAL SEMEN STORAGE UNIT

LIQUID NITROGEN CONTAINER CONSTRUCTION. Liquid nitrogen containers (or units) are like well engineered thermos flasks. They come in different sizes, shapes and prices according to the role for which they are designed. There are basically two types of unit available:

Units designed for use at AB centres. These are characterised by very large storage capacity and large or 'open' necks designed for easy access. They require large quantities of liquid nitrogen and are generally unsuitable for farm use.

'Long life' units designed for farm use. These have 'narrow' necks and hence use small amounts of liquid nitrogen which makes them very suitable for field use. The narrow neck restricts the storage capacity of the unit. However, all of the units available have more than adequate storage capacity for most artificial breeding programs.

MAINTENANCE AND USE OF CONTAINERS. Semen must be stored at a temperature below minus 80°C to avoid deterioration in quality (fertilising capacity). Most units will maintain the temperature at well below minus 80°C with only a few millimetres of liquid nitrogen remaining. However, it is strongly advised that the level of liquid nitrogen never be allowed to fall below 15 cm. This ensures that straws may be removed for insemination while the other straws remain safely stored. The goblets will be full of liquid nitrogen allowing safer removal of straws whilst still keeping stored straws immersed. Goblets will not float out of buckets and empty their straws to the bottom of the unit when the liquid nitrogen is being refilled, and there will be sufficient reserves should unavoidable delays in liquid nitrogen supply occur.

Measurement of liquid nitrogen levels is quite simple. A thin plastic rod or piece of dowel can be used as a dipstick. A frost line will indicate the level of liquid nitrogen if the rod is held in the unit for a short time and then exposed to the atmosphere.

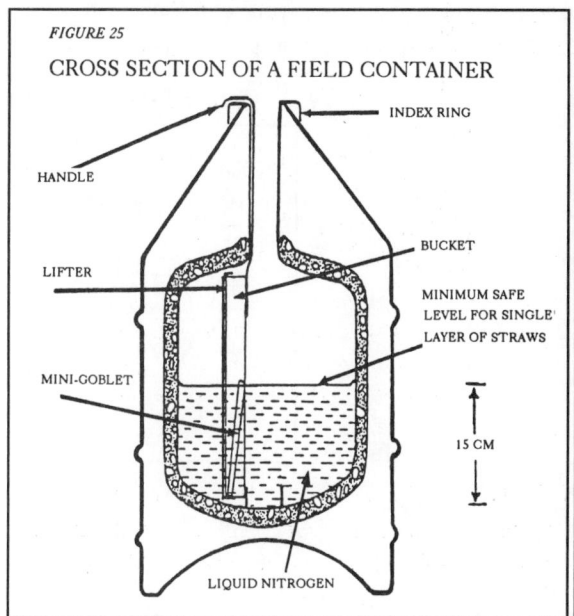

FIGURE 25
CROSS SECTION OF A FIELD CONTAINER

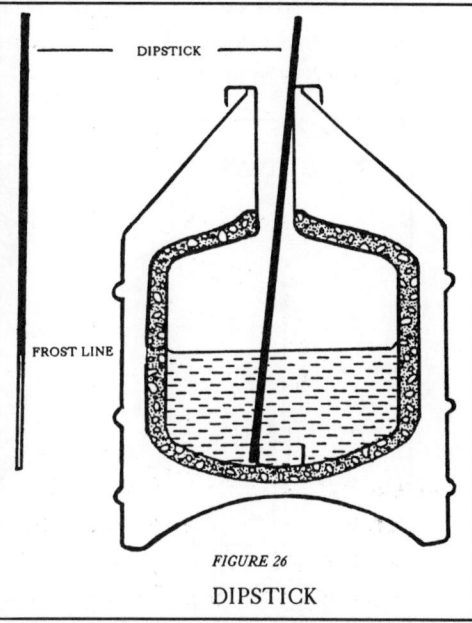

FIGURE 26
DIPSTICK

Knowing when to Top up Liquid Nitrogen

A dipstick can be marked to indicate the level at which a refill of liquid nitrogen should be ordered. It is wise to leave a safety margin when ordering nitrogen. There have been instances when units have run dry because the nitrogen supply was delayed.

One disadvantage of using a dipstick is that its use increases the rate of nitrogen loss and there is some risk to the operator as the liquid nitrogen may boil out of the unit when the warm rod is inserted.

> *Under no circumstances use a metal rod or a hollow rod as a dipstick. A hollow rod is dangerous because boiling will force nitrogen through it and out over a considerable distance.*

An alternative method is to set a critical weight for the unit and weigh it at regular intervals. When the weight of the unit falls to the critical weight, more liquid nitrogen should be ordered.

Perhaps the most satisfactory procedure is to work out the unit's rate of nitrogen consumption and then, after assessing the safe storage period, place reminders to re-order at regular intervals on a calendar.

Units should still be checked periodically to guard against breakdowns or slow leaks. In most cases the weakest point of the unit is in the non-metal neck section. The first and most visible sign is the appearance of a frost, from condensation, on the outside neck of the unit. If semen is to be saved it must be transferred as soon as possible to another unit.

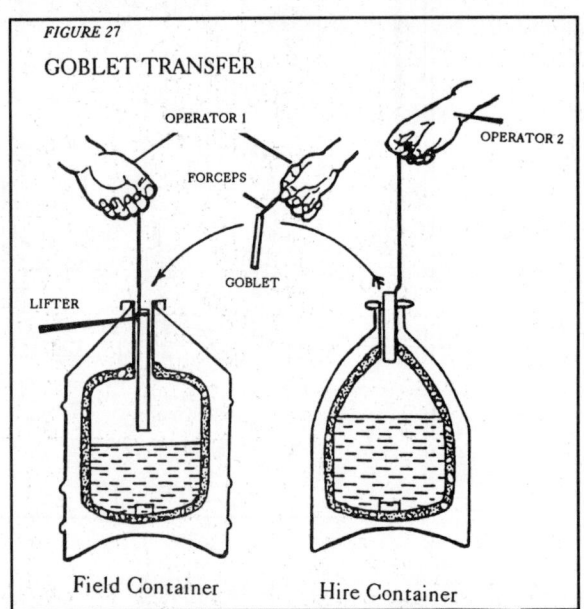

FIGURE 27
GOBLET TRANSFER

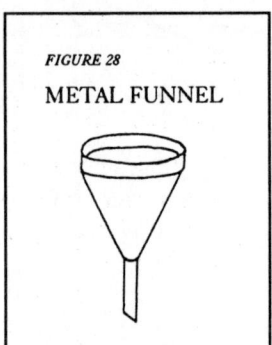

FIGURE 28
METAL FUNNEL

REFILLING PROCEDURES AND FIELD TRANSFER OF SEMEN. Any semen which is ordered will be supplied in 'hire units' which will also contain nitrogen.

1. Place the hire unit close to the farm unit.
2. Determine from the packing slip in which bucket any ordered semen is stored.
3. Determine in which bucket you wish to place the ordered semen.
4. With the aid of another person, raise both buckets, using forceps, and transfer the goblets containing the semen from the hire unit to the farm unit. This must be done carefully.
5. Remove all empty goblets from the farm unit.
6. As soon as possible lower the buckets back into place.
7. After transfer of semen is complete, remove all buckets from the hire unit and with the aid of a metal funnel carefully pour all liquid nitrogen from the hire unit into the farm unit.
8. Replace all buckets in the hire unit and return them as soon as possible to the AB centre.

Plastic funnels will crack or explode and may spill liquid nitrogen.

DRY SHIPPERS. Small quantities of semen or embryos and biological samples may be transported safely in 'dry' shippers. These contain a porous filler which absorbs and stores liquid nitrogen so that there is no actual free liquid to spill. They have only a single bucket so only limited numbers of straws can be transported. They are useful in situations where conventional tanks with free nitrogen are unsuitable.

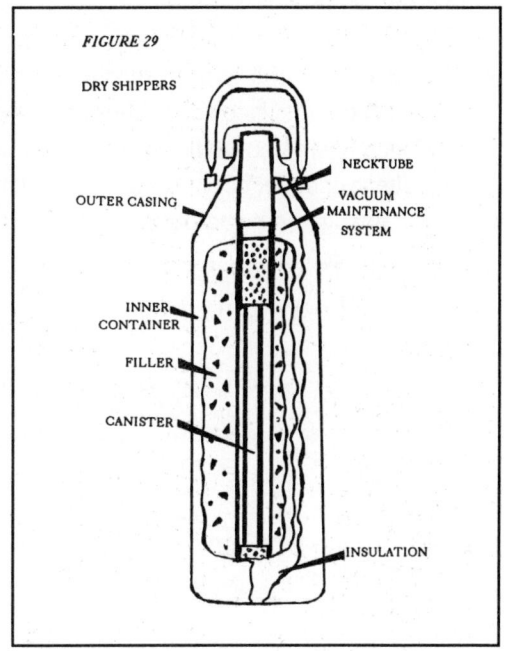

FIGURE 29
DRY SHIPPERS

Points to Consider when Purchasing Liquid Nitrogen Units

There are a number of manufacturers of long life units suitable for farm use—Taylor-Wharton and M.V.E. are the most common brands in Australia.

The advertisements, brochures and technical literature from all companies have common terminology although different standards may be applied to the terms used. Check these standards carefully before comparing the units. The terminology includes:

- static holding time
- working time
- safe storage time
- liquid nitrogen consumption
- storage capacity.

STATIC HOLDING TIME. Static holding time is the time taken for all the liquid nitrogen to evaporate from a stationary unit from which the buckets have been removed and which is not opened. It is of limited value for selecting units, and not to be confused with the period of time for which semen may be safely stored.

WORKING TIME. Working time is the time taken for all the liquid nitrogen to evaporate from a unit in which the buckets are in place and filled with straws of semen. This term also is not to be confused with the period of time for which semen may be safely stored.

The working time will be shorter than the static holding time because the semen and buckets displace some liquid nitrogen. The bucket handles also increase liquid nitrogen evaporation from the unit due to heat transfer from the atmosphere. Frequent use, i.e. opening the unit to withdraw semen, will also markedly increase liquid nitrogen consumption.

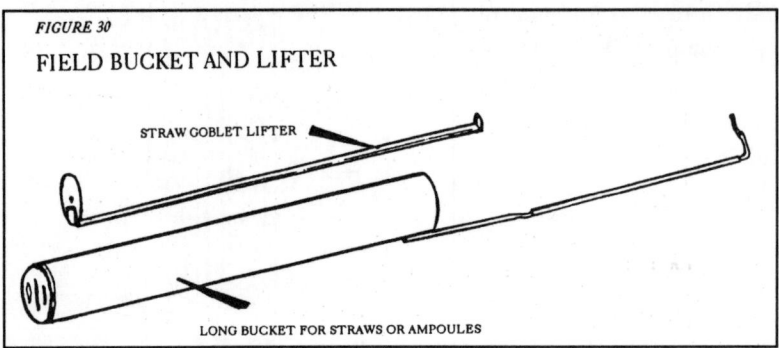

FIGURE 30
FIELD BUCKET AND LIFTER

SAFE STORAGE TIME. 'Safe' storage time is the time taken for the liquid nitrogen level in the unit to fall to 15 cm. This term usually does not appear in promotional material supplied by the manufacturers. Field experience has shown that with normal farm use, the safe storage period is approximately one-half of the quoted static holding time for most units.

LIQUID NITROGEN CONSUMPTION. This figure will be quoted as liquid nitrogen consumption per day. The lower this figure the better. Any unit which uses more than 0·2 L per day is not suitable for field use.

Storage Capacity

Storage capacity of units is affected by the type of bucket and the method of semen packaging. There are two types of buckets available. The short bucket is suitable only for straws. The long bucket is suitable for ampoules in canes or two layers of straws.

Although long buckets may double the storage capacity for straws in the unit, they shorten the safe storage time available if two layers of storage are attempted. Also the bottom layer of straws will remain inaccessible until the top layer has been removed. When selecting semen from the bottom layer a 'lifter' must be used to allow access.

A typical long life unit has approximately the following storage capacities:
- 294 ampoules if using seven ampoule canes
- 480–720 medium straws if using two layers of straws packed into mini-goblets
- 960–1440 mini-straws if using two layers of straws packed into mini-goblets.

In using a single layer bucket, storage capacity is halved. If the straws are packed 'bulk', almost double the quoted number of straws may be stored. Due to handling difficulties, however, this method of storage is not recommended for farm use.

As storage capacity for all long life units is more than adequate for farm use it is not a vital factor in the selection of a unit.

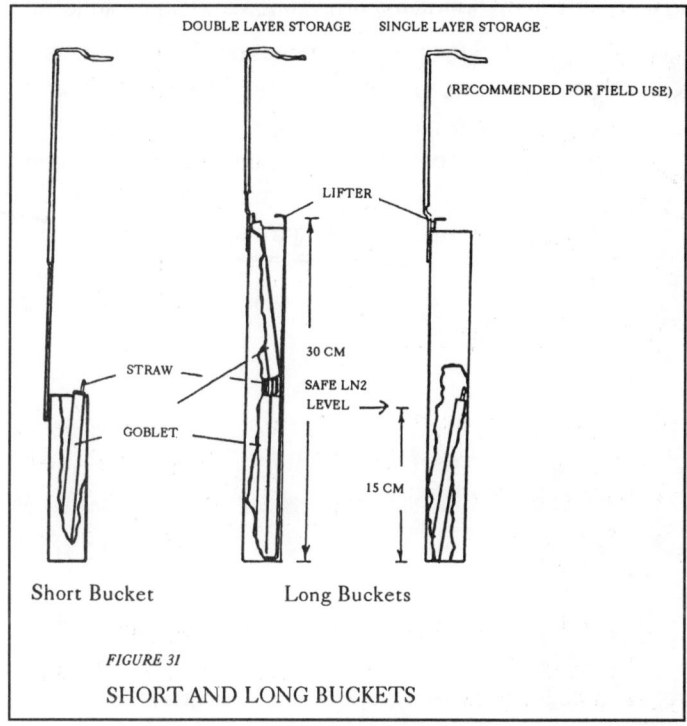

FIGURE 31

SHORT AND LONG BUCKETS

INSEMINATION TECHNIQUE

Semen Handling

Correct semen handling technique is vital in the insemination routine. If maximum conception rates are to be realised, the following procedures should be adhered to.

1. Prepare insemination equipment as near as possible to the inseminating area to avoid undue delays.
2. **Always** prepare insemination equipment in a clear, dry and shaded area. Direct sunlight will injure sperm.

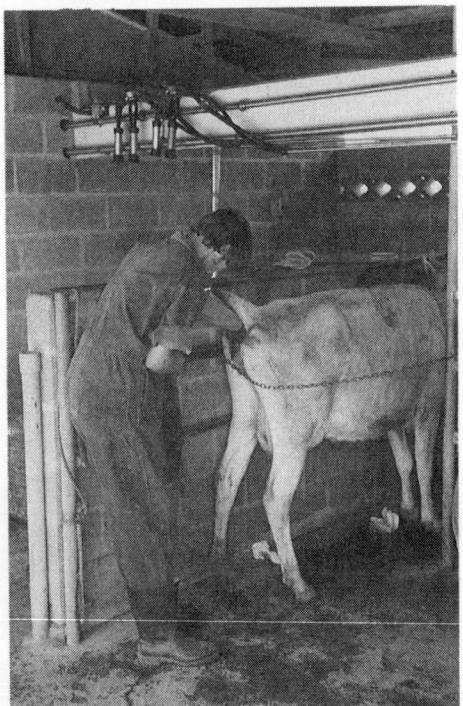

A COVERED BAIL AREA WITH ADEQUATE RESTRAINT IS ESSENTIAL

Complete Farm Kit (for Insemination with Straws)

Long life liquid nitrogen unit
Dipstick for measuring nitrogen level
Metal tool box 50 cm (or more) long (to hold pistolettes and sheaths)
1 (or more) mini-pistolettes with sheaths (pistolettes are sometimes called straw or insemination guns)
1 medium pistolette with sheaths
Straw tweezers

Clean, sharp scissors
Arm length gloves of disposable plastic
Glove lubricant
Thawing flask and thermometer
Paper towel
Record book and semen inventory

The same operation principles and loading procedures apply to both medium and mini-straws.

Mini-guns (or mini-pistolettes) are suitable only for mini-straws i.e. 0·25 cc straws while medium guns and sheaths are suitable only for medium straws i.e. 0·5 cc. Universal sheaths—those with the green adapters—can be used for both mini and medium straws using the appropriate mini-gun or medium gun.

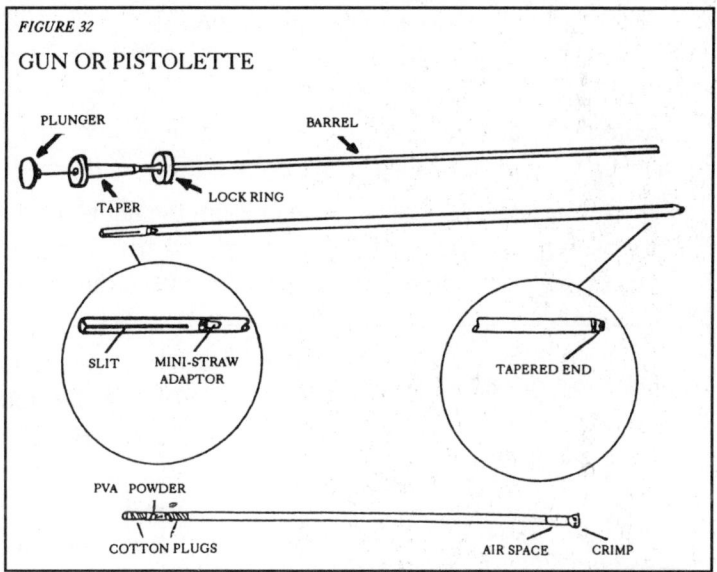

FIGURE 32
GUN OR PISTOLETTE

Loading Straw Guns

1. Identify the bucket containing the required straw or straws by consulting the semen inventory (see previous chapter). Thaw straws only one at a time. Semen should be placed in the cow as soon as practical after removal from liquid nitrogen.
2. Place and prepare the kit box. Check the temperature of the thawing solution (see below under the heading 'Thawing' for information about the thawing solution). The temperature should be 35°C.
3. Lift the handle of the bucket from its notch, place it directly across the neck of the unit so that it now lies opposite its former position, then lift it to the

desired height. Always keep the bucket as low as possible while keeping comfortable access to straws.

4. Remove the straw from the goblet using forceps. Grasp the laboratory end firmly, shake vigorously two or three times and place it immediately in the thawing solution. Shaking removes liquid nitrogen from the cotton wad on the manufacturer's plug and minimises the risk of explosion and/or straw splitting. *The laboratory end is always up in the goblets, the thawing flask and the pistolette.* Avoid undue exposure of semen. Remember straws have no safe exposure time and once removed from liquid nitrogen should be used.

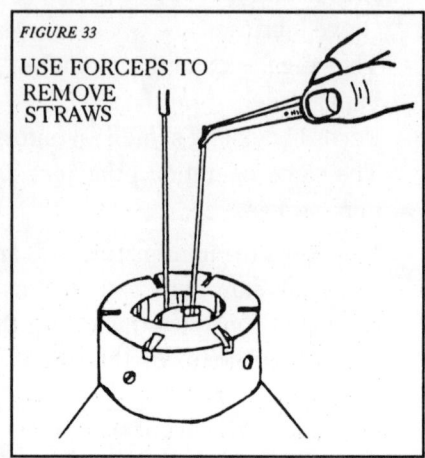

FIGURE 33
USE FORCEPS TO REMOVE STRAWS

When selecting and removing semen, work as far down the neck of the unit as is comfortable, preferably below the frost line. On cold mornings the lifter may be held up by use of a bulldog clip to avoid burning of fingers.

When selecting and removing semen from the liquid nitrogen container always use forceps. If fingers are used there is a risk of burns from cold objects, and also a risk of damaging the semen due to heat transfer from the hands.

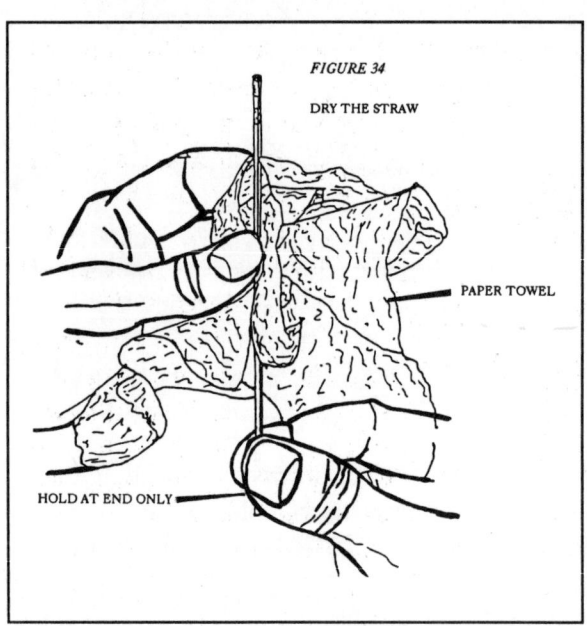

FIGURE 34
DRY THE STRAW

PAPER TOWEL

HOLD AT END ONLY

5. Return the buckets to their correct positions and replace the stopper.
6. Handle the straw only by the ends to avoid temperature fluctuation shock to the sperm. Remove the straw from the thawing solution and dry with towel or paper. Grasp the manufacturer's end (the double wad end) and roll it between thumb and index finger to loosen the wad and facilitate easy ejection of semen. Re-check the name and number of the bull on the straw.

SEMEN HANDLING * 49

7. Remove the gun from its protective case and pull out the plunger to approximately the length of the straw. Place the straw into the insemination gun, manufacturer's end first (laboratory end up). A stop in the barrel prevents the straw going further than the correct distance. Hold the gun and the straw vertically and tap the laboratory end gently with the scissors. This will make the air bubble go as far up towards the laboratory plug as possible.

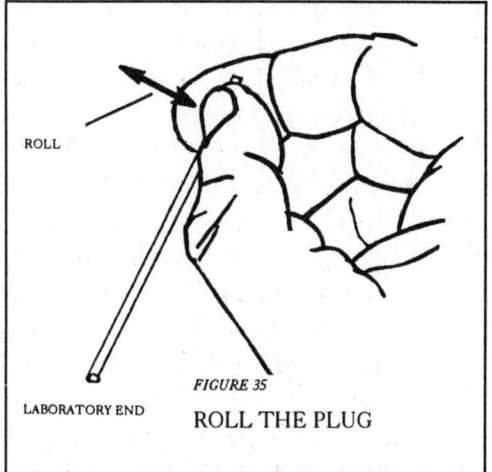

FIGURE 35
ROLL THE PLUG

8. Wipe the scissors. This avoids contamination of the straw about to be cut. Hold the loaded gun vertically at eye level and with scissors make a horizontal cut at 90° to the long axis of the straw through the air bubble, immediately below the laboratory plug or crimp. At least 1 cm of the straw should protrude from the end of the insemination gun. This, together with an accurate cut, is necessary to ensure a perfect seal between the straw and the sheath which is placed over the 'barrel'. Wipe scissor blades after cutting the straw to avoid contaminating the next straw to be cut.

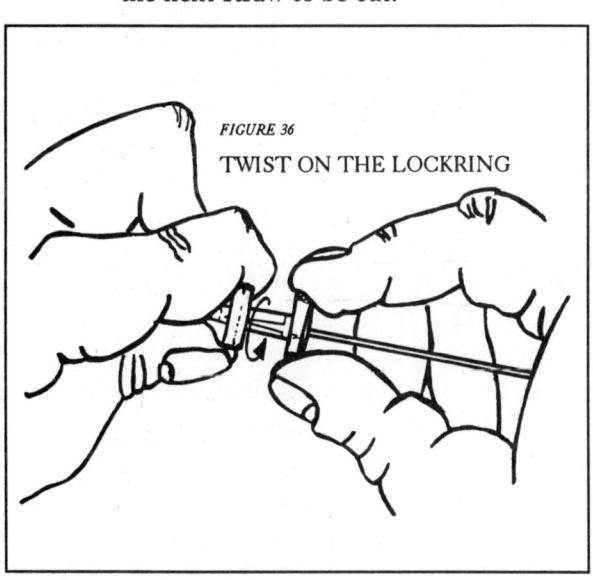

FIGURE 36
TWIST ON THE LOCKRING

9. Remove the sheath from its protective container and place it over the barrel. (Handle only the split end to keep the sheath clean.) Holding the lock ring above the tapered section, push the sheath on over the tapered section and through the lock ring until the end of the straw and the inside edge of the sheath are flush. Twist the lock ring and push it onto the tapered section to lock the sheath into position.

10. Push the plunger in until semen is just visible at the end of the sheath. This shortens the span of the fingers and thumb required when depressing the plunger during insemination. It also removes the chance of carrying contamination from the vagina into the uterus by eliminating the hollow space at

the end of the sheath. Do **not load more than two** guns at any one time.
11. Inseminate the cow as described in section B, below.

After Insemination

1. Loosen the locking ring. Do not allow it to slide onto the soiled part of the sheath.
2. Slide the sheath off the barrel. The straw will be removed with the sheath.
3. Re-check the name and batch number of the bull and record them in the breeding management records.
4. Discard the sheath and straw and dispose of them hygienically.

Preparing Equipment for Insemination with Ampoules or Pellets

The same equipment can be used for both ampoules and pellets. Pellets are drops of diluted frozen semen which are stored in bulk. They are no longer used commercially, since individual doses cannot be identified.

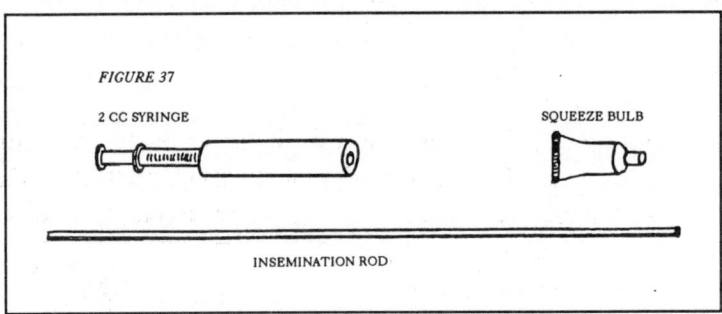

FIGURE 37

1. Place and prepare the kit box. Select semen as for straws. It may be necessary to remove ampoules from canes with fingers.
2. Place the ampoule in thawing solution (iced water).
3. Remove and dry the ampoule thoroughly with a paper towel.
4. Attach the plastic insemination rod to the syringe and adaptor or to a plastic squeeze bulb. When using a syringe make sure that the plunger is not fully depressed, i.e. withdraw it slightly so that 0·25 to 0·5 cc of air is in the syringe.
5. Break the neck of the ampoule. Most ampoules are prescored so that this step is easy. If the ampoule is not scored then score or rasp it lightly with a scoring file. (A nail file may suffice if nothing else is available.)
6. Slowly insert the plastic insemination rod into the ampoule. At the same time carefully withdraw the plunger of the syringe so that semen is drawn up into the insemination rod. Avoid bubbles in the rod. If a plastic squeeze bulb is used, squeeze the bulb prior to insertion of the plastic rod. Slowly release the bulb when inserting the plastic rod so that the semen is drawn up into the rod.
7. Inseminate the cow as per section B, below.
8. Make sure all semen is expelled in the cow using the air reserve left in step 4.

The procedure for pelleted semen is the same as that for ampoules, except that the semen is withdrawn from a container holding the thawed pellet in reconstituting diluent, and not from an ampoule.

UNIVERSAL GUN. The Universal gun can be used for all known methods of semen packaging when used with its blue or 'stiff' sheath (i.e. for ampoules, fresh semen or pellets and similarly packaged semen). The plunger of the gun with the plastic pumping adaptor of the blue sheath forms a piston. This has a syringe like action in the sheath. Semen can be sucked into and expelled from the sheath by withdrawing and depressing the plunger.

The green plugged or universal sheath can be used for all straw systems. The loading procedure is exactly the same as for the standard mini or medium straw guns. However, the tapered section of the barrel is removable allowing the barrel to be reversed to adapt to either mini or medium straws.

When using the universal gun it is essential that the sheath and tapered section be securely locked into place with the locking ring to avoid 'disintegration' of the gun during semen deposition.

Thawing

Research has shown that maximum sperm survival rate is achieved when the thawing procedure is the reverse of the processing and freezing procedure. The processing and freezing steps are a gradual lowering of temperature to minus 196°C.

To achieve the reverse, i.e. a raising of temperature from minus 196°C to 35°C, a thawing solution **must** be used. Fluid achieves a much more rapid thaw than the hottest of air. For this reason, thawing in the air, in gum boots, your mouth or in the cow is **not recommended**. Conception rates will be lowered if semen is not correctly thawed. This applies particularly to bulls whose conception rates are naturally low.

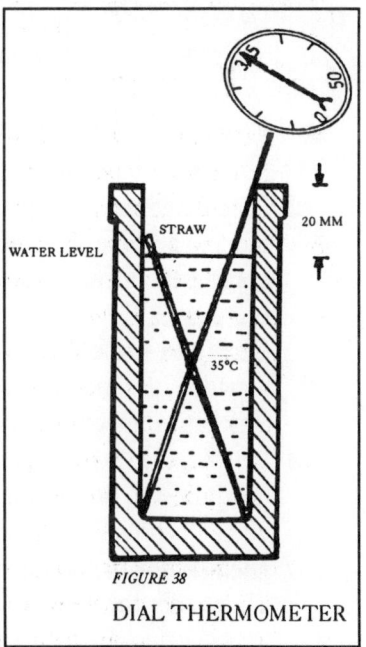

FIGURE 38

DIAL THERMOMETER

Recommended Thawing Procedures

MINI-STRAWS AND MEDIUM STRAWS.

1. Place straws in water of 34°C to 36°C, for a minimum of 30 seconds.
2. Never submerge the straw completely. Leave 1 cm at the laboratory end exposed to avoid the entry of water in case of imperfections during processing.

Baby bottle warmers make ideal thawing flasks.

The temperature must be measured using a thermometer.

AMPOULES. Ampoules should be thawed in iced water (5°C).

Insemination of the Cow

The first attempts at artificial insemination involved deposition of the semen in the vagina, but fertility with this technique was low. Some improvement was achieved with the introduction of the speculum method for insemination, as semen could then be deposited in the cervix. Conception rates were greatly improved following the introduction of the recto-vaginal technique.

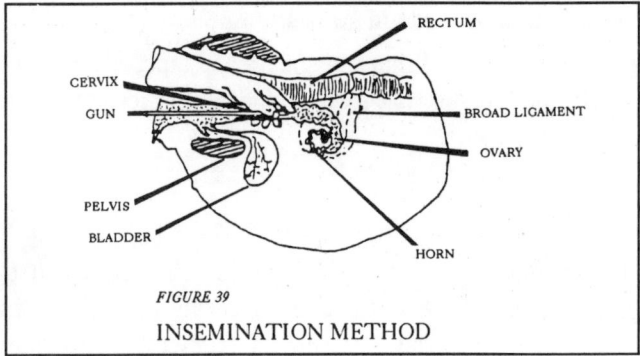

FIGURE 39
INSEMINATION METHOD

In the recto-vaginal technique, an insemination instrument is inserted into the vagina and guided through the cervix by a gloved hand in the rectum controlling and fixing the cervix. This method of insemination is the most efficient in terms of results, labour and hygiene. It should be carried out as follows:

1. Load insemination equipment as indicated in section A, above.
2. Put on a glove and lubricate it with glove lubricant. Try to keep the hand holding the insemination instrument as dry as possible. *Never* load guns with a glove on.
3. Carry the loaded gun in your mouth, to leave both arms free. Avoid contact between the gun and any object near the insemination area. Contamination may cause infection and reduce conception chances.
4. Let the cow know you are there by talking while approaching slowly. Lift the tail, form the fingers into a cone and, with a twisting motion, gently insert your gloved hand into the rectum. Locate the cervix. *Do not force your hand into the cow's rectum as it is possible to rupture it. This could result in the cow's death.*
5. Check that the cow is not pregnant. (Follow the procedure on pages 21-23)

6. Release the cervix and uterus. Remove all traces of faeces and water from the vulva with a piece of paper towel. Spread the fingers of your gloved hand and pull your arm backwards. At the same time push your wrist down and to the left to open the lips of the vulva. The insemination gun can now be inserted with minimal contamination.

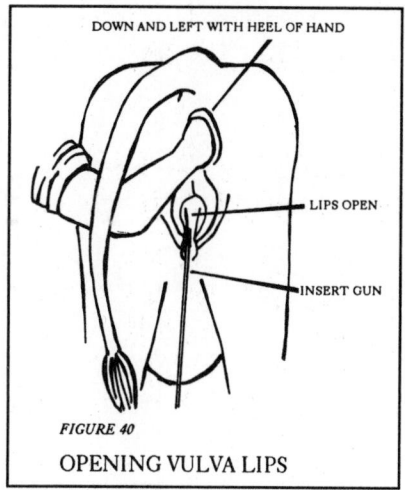

FIGURE 40
OPENING VULVA LIPS

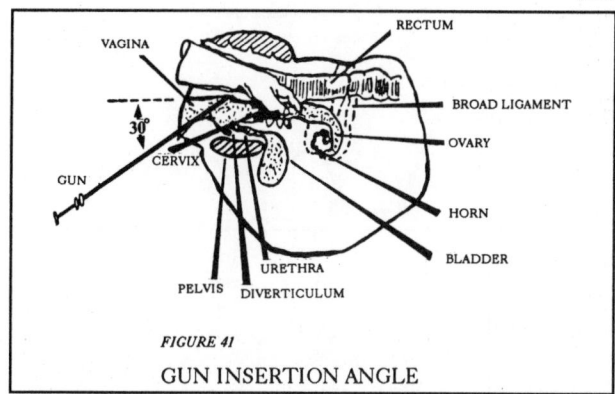

FIGURE 41
GUN INSERTION ANGLE

7. The point of the gun must be introduced at an angle 30° below the horizontal to pass along the top of the vulva and vagina. This avoids the entrance to the urethra and urethral diverticulum which lie on the floor of the vagina.
8. Gently move the gun forward until a distinct grittiness is felt, indicating that the cervix has been reached. If the gun is caught in a vaginal fold it may be necessary to push the cervix forward to straighten out the fold.
9. By manipulation of the cervix and gentle pressure on the gun, it should be possible to guide the tip of the gun through the cervix and into the uterus. The tip can usually be felt through the thinner wall of the uterus. The gun must not be carried further forward than just through the cervix (1 cm at the most). *The maximum pressure which should be placed on the gun is that which can be obtained when holding the gun with the thumb and one finger.*

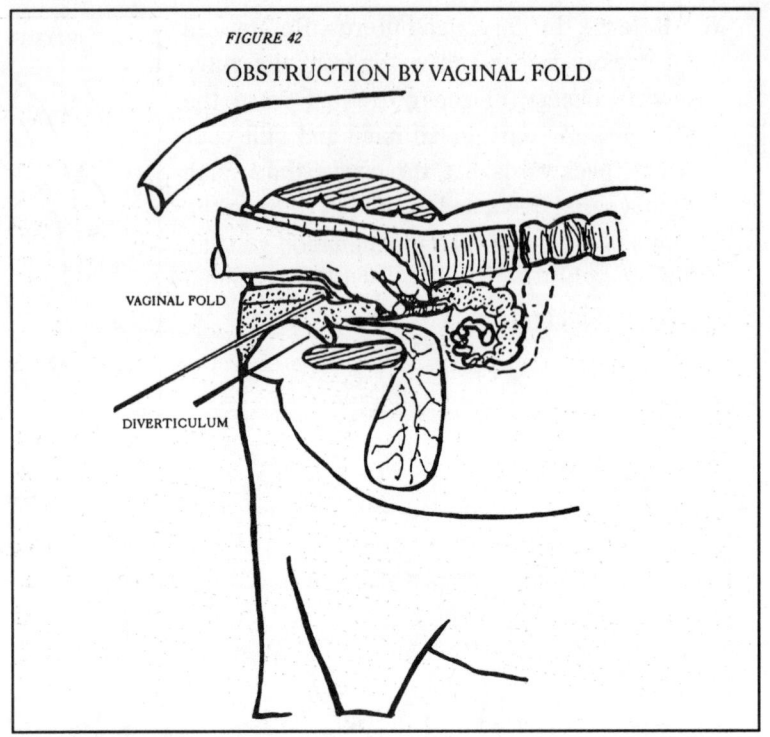

FIGURE 42
OBSTRUCTION BY VAGINAL FOLD

VAGINAL FOLD

DIVERTICULUM

FIGURE 43
PUSHING TO STRAIGHTEN VAGINAL FOLDS

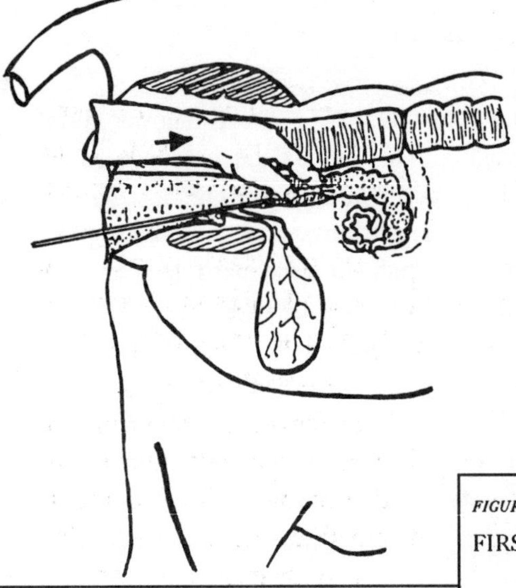

FIGURE 44
FIRST DEPOSITION SITE

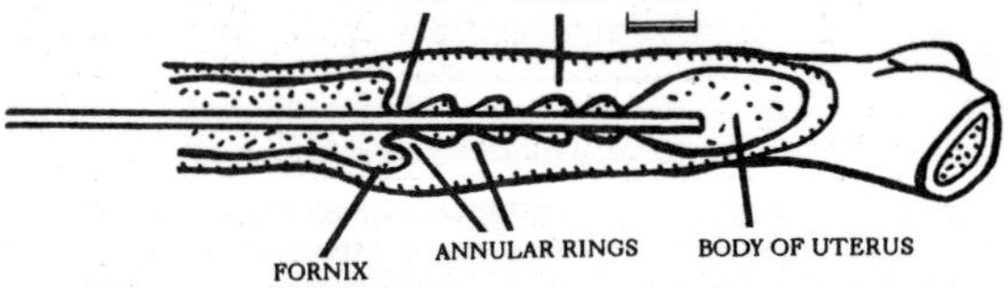

OS CERVIX 1 CM

FORNIX ANNULAR RINGS BODY OF UTERUS

With repeat cows (i.e. cows returning on heat), many sources recommend placing the gun only up to the *middle of the cervix* because up to 3% of pregnant cows may cycle at 3 and 6 weeks. Intra-uterine insemination may be harmful in these cases. Mid-cervical insemination is much safer.

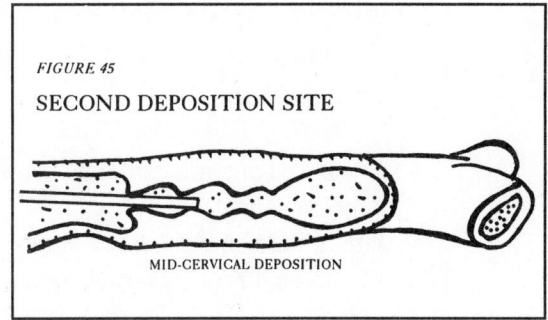

FIGURE 45

SECOND DEPOSITION SITE

MID-CERVICAL DEPOSITION

10. Slowly deposit half to two-thirds of the semen in the body of the uterus and the remainder in the middle of the cervix.
11. Remove the gun from the tract and massage the cervix and uterus for a few seconds to stimulate the release of oxytocin. Rough handling upsets the cow and causes the release of adrenalin which counteracts the effect of oxytocin.
12. Loosen the locking ring of the gun but do not allow it to slide onto the soiled part of the sheath. Slide the sheath off the barrel. The straw will come away with the sheath. Do not discard the sheath and straw until records have been completed. Burn the sheath and straw and disposable glove to avoid possible disease transmission.
13. Release the cow from the bail or crush.
14. Observe personal hygiene measures by washing in disinfectant and cleaning boots. Maintain equipment properly. Dismantle guns for cleaning and wash them in methylated spirits.

Timing of Insemination

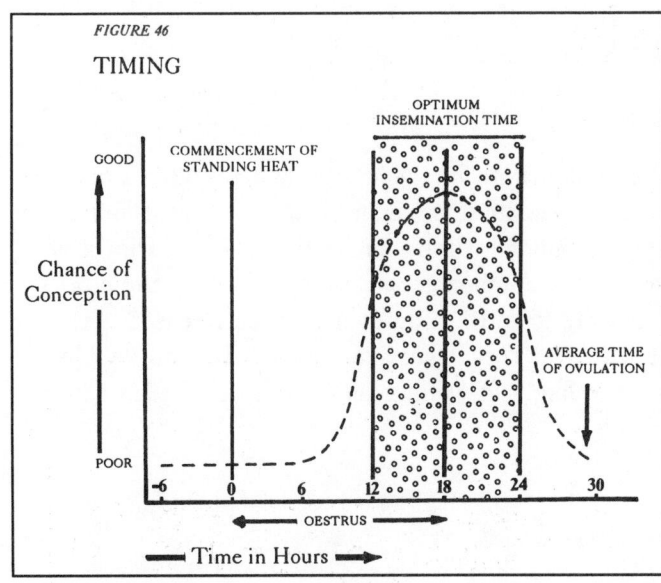

FIGURE 46 TIMING

Correct timing of insemination is as important as correct placement of semen. Field experience has shown that the best results are obtained when the insemination is performed at or near the end of oestrus.

The beginning and end of oestrus are very difficult to determine. The simplest practical method of timing inseminations is to use the a.m.–p.m. rule.

Cows first seen on heat	Insemination Time
Morning (a.m.)	Same Afternoon (p.m.)
Afternoon (p.m.)	Next Morning (a.m.)

- Two-thirds of cows commence oestrus at night and so will first be seen on heat in the morning.
- With heifers and some *Bos indicus* breeds, many authorities do not recommend the a.m.–p.m. rule. They recommend that these animals should be inseminated soon after the first observed oestrus.

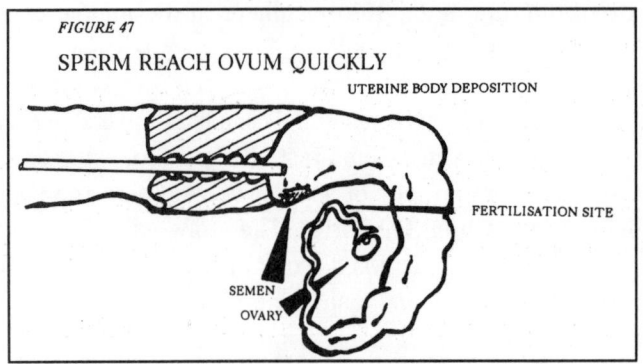

FIGURE 47
SPERM REACH OVUM QUICKLY

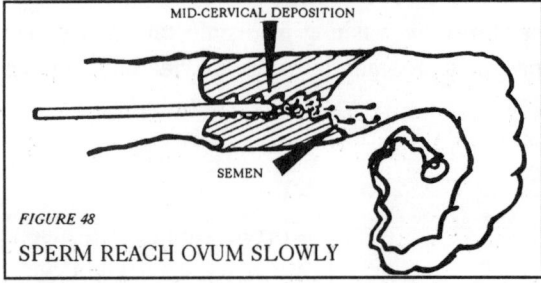

FIGURE 48
SPERM REACH OVUM SLOWLY

Dual Placement of Semen

The reason that placement of semen both in the uterus and the cervix is recommended (see step 10 in the insemination procedure above) is that it helps to overcome the unpredictability of ovulation times. In cattle, ovulation can occur from 2 to 26 hours after the end of heat. Semen deposited in the body of the uterus reaches the fertilisation site quickly to fertilise an ovum that is released earlier than normal. Semen deposited in the cervix survives longer. Due to its slow release from the cervix it is more likely to fertilise an ovum released later than normal.

Hygiene

Hygiene precautions are observed to minimise, if not eliminate, the physical transfer of infective disease agents:

- between farms
- between animals
- from animals to humans
- into the cervix and uterus
- from miscellaneous sources.

PREVENTING TRANSMISSION BETWEEN FARMS. Protective clothing. If possible wear rubber footwear and either overalls or a cape on the farm. If this clothing becomes soiled it can be cleaned more readily than ordinary clothes. Use disposable plastic overshoes on farms which are known to have a disease problem.

Washing. Scrub buckets and boots, paying particular attention to the tread on the sole.

Chemical agents. Use soap and/or antiseptics to improve the efficiency of all cleansing procedures.

Towels. Use disposable paper towels.

Minimise equipment. Take the minimum of equipment into the dairy or shed. The more items carried, the greater is the likelihood of transmitting infective agents. Apart from the bucket and scrubbing brush, all items should be carried in an equipment box.

PREVENTING TRANSMISSION BETWEEN ANIMALS. Use disposable equipment once only. Do not split straws or re-use sheaths or insemination rods. When more than one cow is to be inseminated, the technician should use a fresh disposable glove for each insemination.

PREVENTING TRANSMISSION FROM ANIMALS TO HUMANS. Gloves. The use of long 'obstetric gloves' is recommended. If gloves are not worn there is a strong possibility of serious infection occurring even though soap and/or antiseptics may be used for thorough washing immediately after insemination. Cuts and abrasions on the hands may permit the entry of infection.

Don't smoke. Smoking while handling contaminated insemination equipment is a sure way of transmitting infection to humans.

PREVENTING TRANSMISSION INTO CERVIX AND UTERUS. Clean the vulva. Cleaning of the vulva prior to introduction of the insemination gun should receive careful attention. When gross contamination is present, a clean paper towel should be used for a final cleaning. Ensure the lips of the vulva are closed during cleaning to prevent faecal material entering the vagina.

Open the vulva. No matter how thoroughly the vulva is cleaned, the area will never be sterile. For this reason it is essential that the lips of the vulva be parted to permit free entry of the tip of the insemination gun. Opening of the vulva is part of step 6 of the insemination procedure above.

Opening the vulva can generally be achieved by wrist pressure directed downwards and to the left. With some cows it may be necessary to draw the cervix back and/or stroke the wall of the rectum before applying wrist pressure.

These methods prevent introduction of the insemination gun into the suburethral diverticulum. If they don't work and no assistance is available, place a piece of paper or cotton wool into the vulva so that it remains open enough to allow clean entry of the gun.

MISCELLANEOUS SOURCES OF INFECTIONS. **Interference by pets or children**. Take precautions to ensure dogs, cats and children will not interfere with insemination equipment that is left unattended.

Accidental contact. Avoid contact between the insemination gun and shed walls, posts, rails, switching tails, etc.

Dirty insemination guns. Clean insemination guns regularly. Dismantle them and wash them in methylated spirits or boil for 10 minutes. Reassemble only when dry. Do *not* simply wash in water or disinfectant as this will lead to gumming up or corrosion of the gun.

Dust. Avoid unnecessarily dusty conditions. Make sure the hammermill or other dusty equipment are not going to be used during insemination.

Faults in AI Technique

Serious faults in insemination technique have been encountered among technicians with many years experience as well as among those recently trained. The insemination of a cow is a complex operation and should be treated as such. By far the biggest cause of faults is complacency.

Overexposure of Semen

Frozen semen has a critical temperature of minus 80°C. If the temperature of the dose is raised above this level and re-frozen, sperm will be damaged. Ampoules allow a considerable safety margin, and exposure for 30 seconds is acceptable as long as sufficient time is allowed for re-freezing.

The only time a straw should be removed from liquid nitrogen is when it is transferred from the container to the thawing solution. There is no safe exposure

time for straws. There are some basic rules to observe to avoid overexposure.
- Avoid raising the bucket above the frost line in the neck of the unit.
- Use forceps to handle straws, working as far down in the unit as possible.
- **Never** identify a straw by exposing it to read the bull's name. Identify semen by markings on mini-goblets and by an index for the container. If an individual straw has to be examined, handle it with forceps under liquid nitrogen. Place the mini-goblet in a bath of nitrogen and ensure that all the straws are covered by the liquid. Remove the straw from the goblet but keep it under the liquid. Bring the dose close to the surface to identify it. Do not raise it above the level of the liquid.
- **Always** lower the canister back into position as soon as the dose has been removed and placed in the thawing solution. Replace the lid immediately.
- Make all movements swift and precise when handling frozen semen.
- **Never** allow the level of liquid to fall below the tops of the mini-goblets. This level provides a margin of safety and avoids the inconvenience of goblets floating out of the canisters when the unit is refilled.
- **Never** remove semen from the liquid nitrogen unit prior to restraining cows.

Incorrect Site of Semen Deposition

Inability to pass an insemination gun through the cervix, or difficulty in doing so, is primarily due to inexperience. A greater and far more common mistake is to pass the gun too far into the uterus. This fault is prevalent, irrespective of experience, and is caused solely by inattention to detail.

The best fertility is obtained by depositing half to two-thirds of the semen in the uterine body and the remaining semen in the middle of the cervix.

Since the uterine body is only 2 to 5 cm in length, uterine depositions must be made *just through the cervix* (see 'Insemination of the Cow', above). Rapid sperm migration to both oviducts is facilitated by deposition in the body of the uterus.

Sperm deposited in the cervix survive longer than sperm deposited in the uterus. Therefore partial cervical deposition is advantageous for cows in early oestrus, and for cows having delayed ovulation.

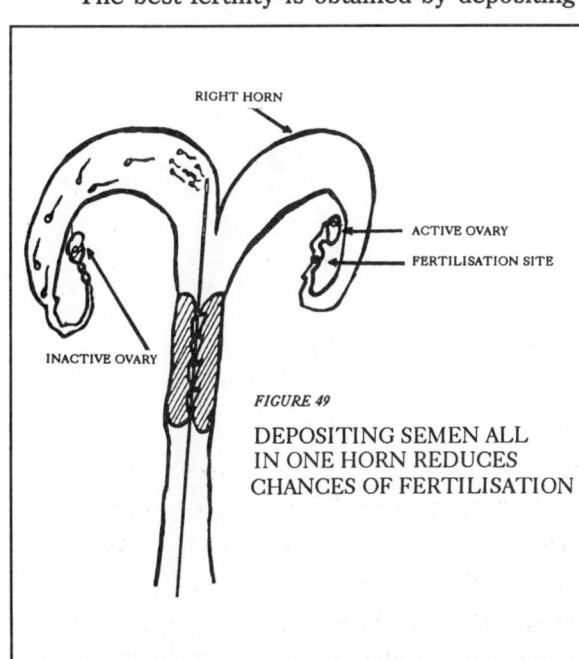

FIGURE 49
DEPOSITING SEMEN ALL IN ONE HORN REDUCES CHANCES OF FERTILISATION

Passing an insemination gun too far through the cervix reduces fertility because:

- All the semen is likely to be in one horn, which lessens the chance of sperm migrating to both oviducts.
- Laceration of the extremely delicate endometrium is likely, even when organs are handled gently. Blood is spermicidal.

The use of force to overcome difficulty in passing the insemination gun through the cervix is a frequent cause of laceration. This may lead to sterility because of adhesions. *Finger and thumb pressure* on the insemination gun is the maximum that should be used. If the gun cannot be manipulated through the cervix, then all semen should be deposited in the middle of the cervix.

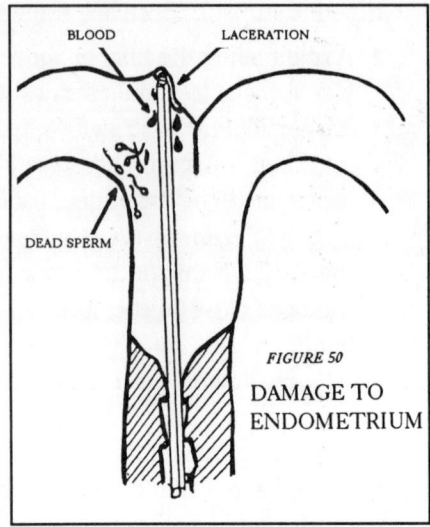

FIGURE 50
DAMAGE TO ENDOMETRIUM

The placement of the gun is best checked through the side walls of the body of the uterus with the index finger and thumb from opposing sides, or with the index finger from underneath.

After insemination always check the tip of the sheath and straw for the presence of blood. This can be done whilst massaging the cervix after insemination.

When feeling for the gun the index finger should not be placed on top of the soft wall of the uterus as the finger may push the sharp tip of the gun into the uterus wall and cause it to bleed.

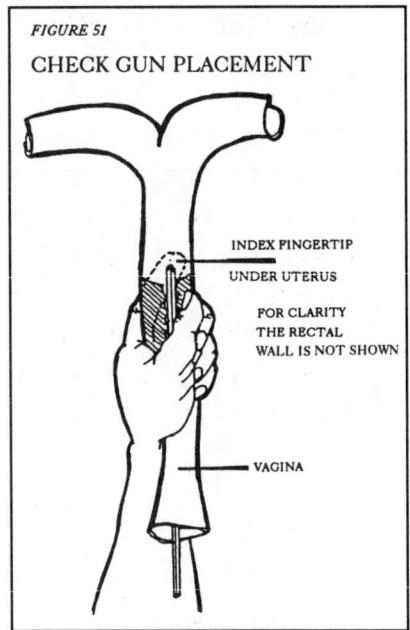

FIGURE 51
CHECK GUN PLACEMENT

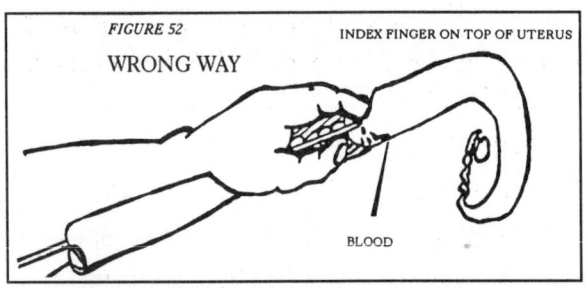

FIGURE 52
WRONG WAY

Rough handling and poor technique may cause the rectum to balloon, making it impossible to manipulate the cervix successfully. Removal of the ballooning may be attempted by placing one or two fingers through the constricting ring at the end of the ballooned area and gently massaging. This may induce the rectum to

FAULTS IN AI TECHNIQUE * 61

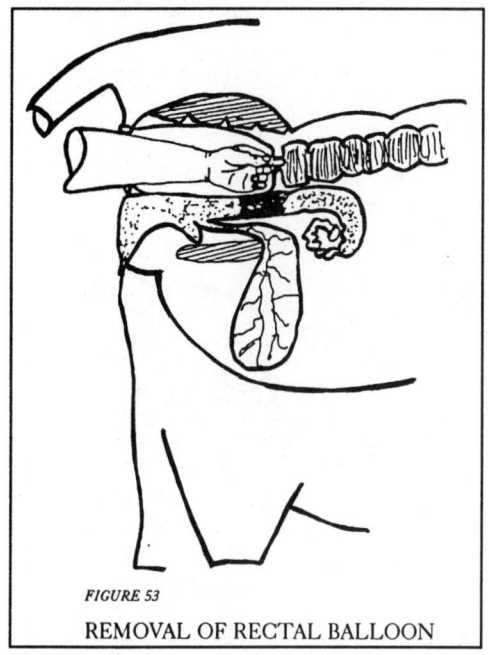

FIGURE 53
REMOVAL OF RECTAL BALLOON

contract and blow the offending air, together with some faeces, out past the arm of the operator, resulting in relaxation of the rectal wall and giving the operator a good opportunity to grasp the cervix. This technique may also be used to clear faeces from the rectum.

Poor Seal Between Straw and Sheath

If the gun is loaded incorrectly some semen will escape into the sheath and perhaps into the barrel. This reduces the number of sperm available for fertilisation. Inspect the equipment after insemination to ensure that your loading procedure is correct.

After loading, the tip of the sheath should be carefully examined for cracks. There have been cases where straws have been pushed through the sheath and into the tract when deposition was attempted.

Sheaths which have been exposed to sunlight will become brittle, crack and shrink. All faulty sheaths should be discarded.

There may be back flushing of semen into the vagina and an uneven distribution of the semen if the plunger is not pushed in slowly and smoothly. Failure to loosen

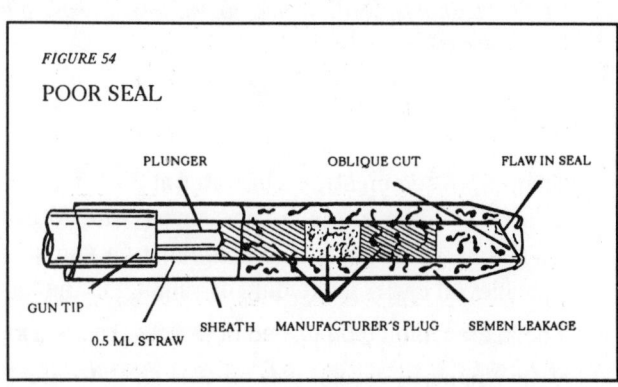

FIGURE 54
POOR SEAL

the manufacturer's plug by rolling before loading the gun may make depression of the plunger difficult.

Neglecting to Open the Vulva

Opening the vulva before the introduction of the gun is a hygiene precaution of major importance. Irrespective of the cleaning precautions practised, there will be heavy bacterial contamination of the vulva. Transfer of bacteria directly into the uterus is therefore inevitable unless the vulva is opened adequately.

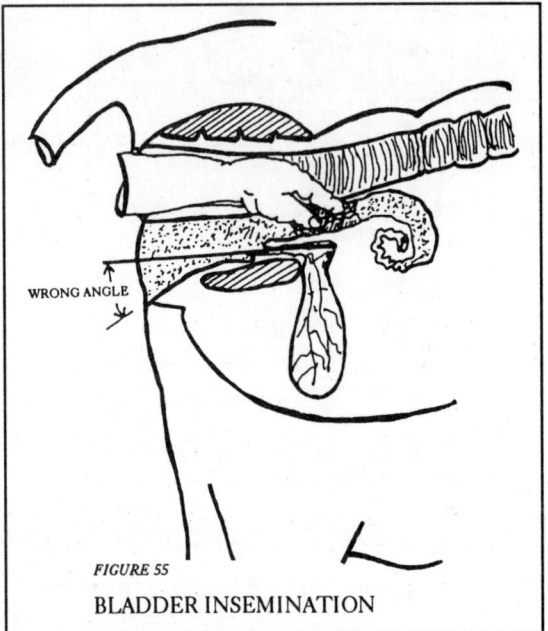

FIGURE 55
BLADDER INSEMINATION

In most cases pressure backwards, downwards and to the left with the wrist (for operators with their left arm in the rectum), will adequately part the lips of the vulva. Alternative approaches for difficult cows are:

- to draw the cervix backwards as wrist pressure is applied
- to move the hand slowly back and forth in the rectum several times before applying wrist pressure
- to massage the cervix and uterus before attempting to open the vulva.

> Drawing the cervix backwards as wrist pressure is applied increases the likelihood of passing the gun into the urethra. Particular care must therefore be taken to ensure that the insemination gun is introduced at an angle 30° below the horizontal. Drawing the cervix backwards will also form folds in the vagina. Consequently, the cervix has to be pushed forward once the gun has been introduced to the vestibule of the vagina.

Thawing

Thawing of semen straws in water at 35°C is recommended because sperm revival is increased due to the faster thawing rate. During cold weather when straws are thawed in warm water, the insemination gun should also be warmed up. This can be achieved easily by holding or rubbing in the hands.

The semen should be placed in the cow as soon as possible after thawing.

Straws must be carefully dried after thawing and before loading the gun.

BULL SELECTION

Basic Genetics

An animal is composed of cells which vary greatly in shape and function. Most cells contain a central body known as the nucleus and within this nucleus are thread like structures called chromosomes. Cattle have 30 pairs, making 60 individual chromosomes. Located on the chromosomes are genes, the basic units which control an animal's appearance and performance.

Growth of tissues in the body depends on cells dividing. The process is known as 'mitosis' and involves:

- a doubling of the number of chromosomes in the cell;
- splitting of the nucleus into two parts, each containing pairs of chromosomes identical to those in the original cell; and
- constriction through the middle of the cell and complete division to form two new cells each identical to the original cell.

The cells of reproduction, the ovum and sperm, are produced by a different form of

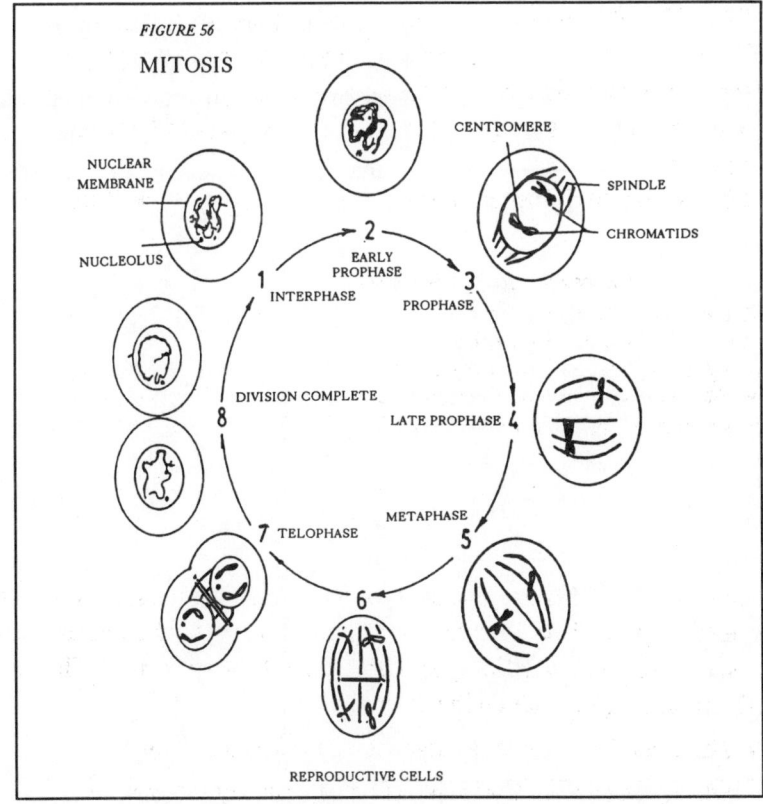

FIGURE 56
MITOSIS

64 * BULL SELECTION

division called 'meiosis'. This process is confined to the ovary and testis. The cells divide but the chromosomes do not undergo the initial doubling. This results in cells with only half the original number of chromosomes.

- The nucleus splits into two parts. (In cattle, each part contains 30 individual chromosomes.)
- The nuclei move to opposite ends of the cell.
- The cell constricts and divides in the middle to form two new cells which are different from the original cell in that the new cells contain only half the chromosomes of the original cell.

When fertilisation occurs in cattle, the 30 individual chromosomes of the sperm unite with the 30 individual chromosomes of the egg to produce a zygote which has the normal chromosome complement, i.e. 30 pairs. This is the basis of inheritance whereby the offspring

FIGURE 57
MEIOSIS

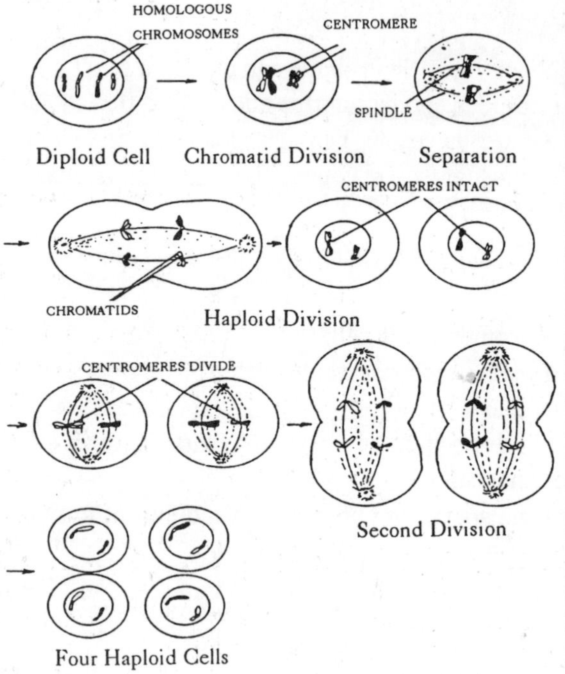

FIGURE 58
SEX DETERMINATION

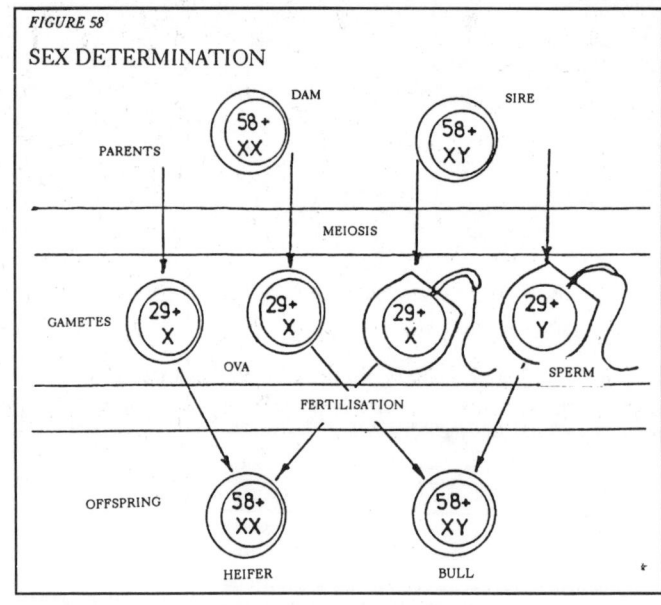

receives half its chromosomes from the sire and half from the dam.

The sex of an animal, like its appearance, is determined by its chromosomes. Of the 30 pairs, one pair, termed 'the sex chromosomes', determines the sex. In females the individuals of a pair are identical and are called X chromosomes. In males one is an X, or female type, and the other is a Y, or male type.

It is very difficult to tell the X from the Y sperm. The Y carriers are thought to be slightly larger and more active thereby causing more male embryos to be conceived. In early pregnancy male embryos appear to be weaker than females and early embryo deaths tend to equalise the ratio of males to females at birth.

There is at present no commercial method of separating the X and Y sperm. This may be possible in the future, enabling the predetermination of the sex of calves.

Basic Selection Principles

Individuals in any population exhibit various traits to a greater or lesser extent than the average for the population. Plotting the distribution of animals according to the degree for which they exhibit a trait produces a distribution curve for that population. For example, a live weight distribution which would be close to what scientists call a 'normal' distribution or 'bell curve'.

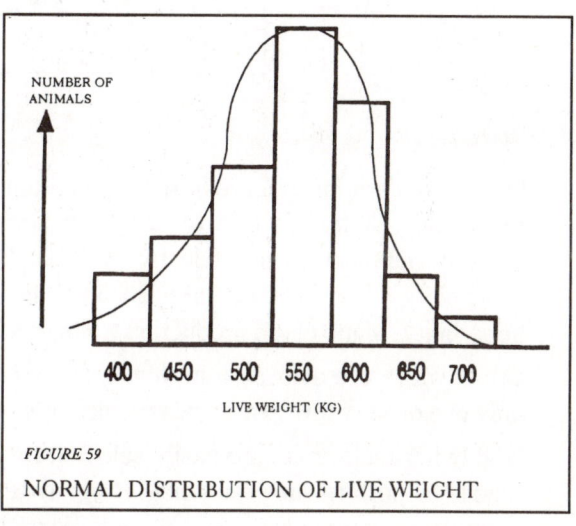

FIGURE 59
NORMAL DISTRIBUTION OF LIVE WEIGHT

Genetic improvement can only be achieved by breeding from superior animals and by culling low producers.

The progeny of the superior breeding stock will also exhibit a normal distribution for a particular trait. However, if top bulls are mated to top cows, the average performance of their progeny will be better than the average for the herd. Some calves will be better than their parents, most will be approximately the same, and others will be worse.

These graphs indicate that most below average progeny of superior parents will be better than the herd average. The aim of selection is to increase the average performance of progeny.

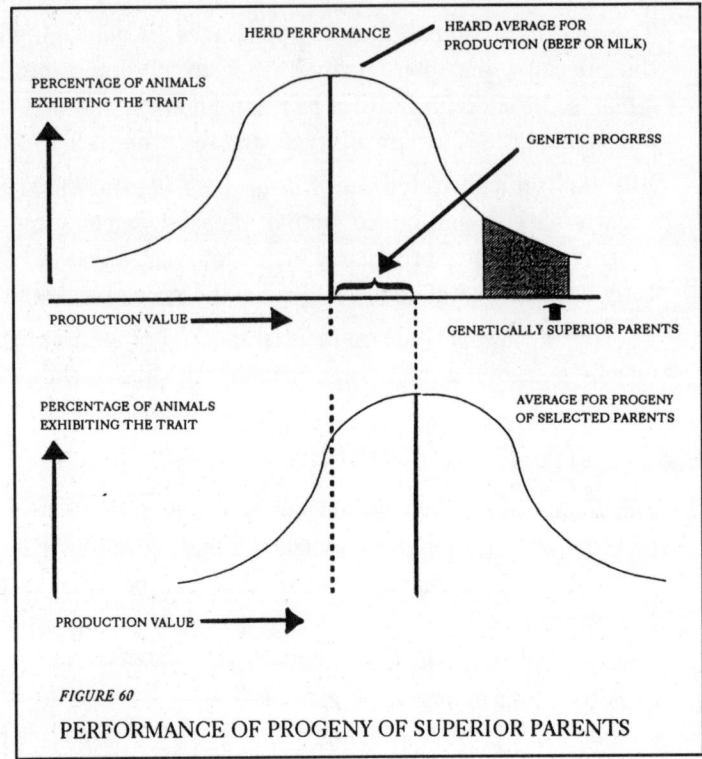

FIGURE 60
PERFORMANCE OF PROGENY OF SUPERIOR PARENTS

Heritability

Some traits are much more heritable than others—i.e. more likely to be passed on to progeny. A trait is said to have low heritability if it is up to 30% heritable. Fertility and most of the productive traits in dairy cattle are in the range of 20–25% heritability. Traits which are 30–50% heritable are said to be of medium heritability. Many of the production traits of beef cattle are in this category.

Traits which are over 50% heritable are of high heritability. Traits which involve only one or very few genes such as coat colour and polledness are amongst them.

Highly heritable traits are easily selected for and breeding stock can be identified readily by performance recording. Progeny testing may be needed for traits of low or moderate heritability to ensure genetic progress. (See the following section.)

FACTORS DETERMINING GENETIC PROGRESS. The rate of genetic progress is determined by several factors. These include:
- the heritability of a characteristic
- culling rates (selection intensity)
- the generation interval
- the number of traits being selected for.

The rate of genetic progress decreases as the number of traits selected for increases. It is, therefore, essential to select only for traits with economic significance.

Dairy Bull Selection; Progeny Testing and ABVs

The most important reason for using AI at present is to facilitate the identification of superior bulls and to then allow their widespread use.

Obviously a bull cannot be milked to determine its genetic worth. Similarly eye appraisal gives very little indication of productive capability. A study of a bull's pedigree may give some indication of merit—bulls with high producing sisters, mothers and grandmothers have a good chance of possessing and passing on the genes for high production.

The only way an accurate measure of genetic worth can be obtained for a dairy bull is to test his progeny i.e. to milk his daughters and measure their production. Progeny testing or 'Bull Proving' schemes for dairy sires are conducted throughout many parts of the world.

Genetic Ratings for Dairy Sires in Australia

In Australia, dairy sires are rated for genetic merit using ABVs (Australian Breeding Values). These ratings are determined by the ADHIS (Australian Dairy Herd Improvement Scheme) which uses the BLUP (best linear unbiased predictor) method of computer analysis for calculating each bull's 'proof' or ABV.

The BLUP analysis considers not only the production of a bull's daughters but also the production of all known relatives. The more information analysed, the better the estimate of genetic merit obtained as expressed in the ABVs. The BLUP method is the most reliable and accurate in the world for assessing genetic merit.

The ADHIS gives ABVs to each Holstein (Holstein-Friesian) sire and Jersey sire that has 20 or more daughters milking in five or more separate herds. These herds have to be 'herd recorded' or production recorded herds.

For other breeds ABVs are issued for sires with ten or more daughters in three or more herds.

Production Trait ABVs

There are five production traits analysed by the ADHIS:
1. total protein yield (in kilograms)
2. total fat yield (in kilograms)
3. total milk yield (in litres)
4. protein percentage
5. fat percentage.

PROTEIN YIELD, FAT YIELD AND MILK YIELD. These are expressed in kilograms of protein and fat and litres of milk above or below the breed base average. The breed base average or zero point was calculated from the average (weighted by daughter numbers) for AI sires' daughters that had completed a lactation up to the 1980–81 herd recording year. In other words the artificial breeding sire average was effectively rated as zero for all traits for the first proofs released in 1982.

For example: Rothrock Cleitus Stefan more commonly known by his NASIS secondary code as STEFAN (Nasis Primary Code 15FFH08) had for the May 1994 ABVs a proof as follows:

    Protein   +38 kg
    Fat   + 56 kg
    Milk   +1698 L

This means that STEFAN daughters on average produced 1698 L more milk, 38 kg more protein and 56 kg more fat per lactation than the average AB sire's daughters of the 1982 ABVs.

When calculating ABVs all lactations of a bull's daughters are considered but the first lactation is the most useful in the calculations. This is because for subsequent lactations a large proportion of a bull's lower producing daughters may have been culled. Consequently when calculating ABVs, the first lactation information is given an increased 'weight'.

PROTEIN AND FAT PERCENTAGES. Protein and fat percentages are expressed as +(plus) or -(minus) i.e. above or below the zero base average for the 1982 ABVs. Provided the test percentage ABV for a bull is higher than the cow he is mated to, the test percentage in the progeny should increase.

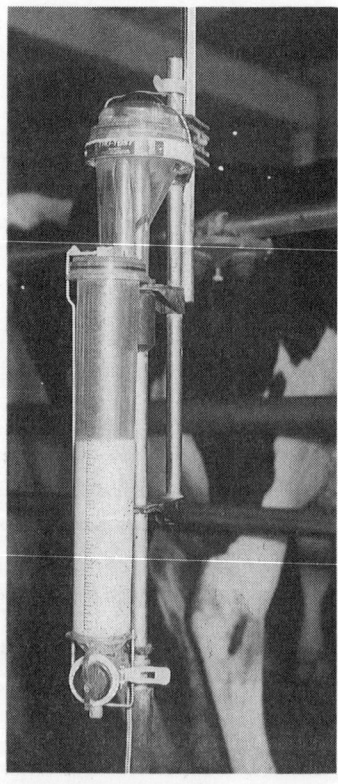

FIRST LACTATION IS THE MOST IMPORTANT FOR ABV CALCULATION.

RELIABILITY. Reliability is a percentage figure often quoted with the ABV data. This gives an indication of the likelihood of a bull's ABV changing with additional information being available in the calculation of the next proof. The more daughters a bull has milking in as many different herds as possible, the more information is available when calculating the ABVs for the bull. This means the proof is more reliable and has a smaller chance of changing (either up or down) than the proof for a bull with fewer daughters and therefore less information.

A bull with thousands of daughters in many different herds may have a reliability of 99% (there is no such thing as a 100% reliability) and there is only an exceedingly small chance of change of his ABVs with additional information.

ABVs for Other Traits

Whilst the ABVs for production traits are the most important—because dairy farmers get paid for producing milk and protein and fat—some other traits do have economic benefits. Workability traits, calving ease and survivability can affect the profitability of dairy cows.

WORKABILITY TRAITS. Workability traits include milking speed, temperament and likeability. These are scored by the farmers milking the cows on an A to E rating. A is very desirable and E is highly undesirable. The results will be expressed as a percentage of a bull's daughters being satisfactory for a particular trait. The range usually extends from 70% satisfactory up to above 90%. It must be noted that even very good bulls will have some unsatisfactory (i.e. D or E) daughters.

CALVING EASE. Calving ease ABVs are based on farmers' assessments of the level of difficulty experienced with the birth of the progeny of a bull.

At this stage only calvings of second or later lactation cows are considered even though the majority of calving difficulties occurs on the first calf. The ABV is expressed as a percentage of cows which experience calving difficulties. It sometimes takes a few years before some AI bulls obtain calving ease ABVs because considerable numbers are needed for sufficient reliability.

SURVIVABILITY ABVS. Survivabilities are reported as the percentage of a bull's daughters surviving from year to year relative to the average performance of AI sires' daughters surviving from one year to the next. For example, if a bull has a survival ABV of ten, then it can be expected that 5% more of his daughters will be in the herd than the average artificial breeding sire's. This is because the score for the average sire is zero; the ABV of ten is a percentage figure, but it is halved to 5% because the sire supplies only half an offspring's genes.

Type Trait ABVs

Type ABVs are available in Australia for the Holstein, Illawarra and Jersey breeds. Breed society classifiers score first lactation heifers of the various bulls in

STRONG CENTRE LIGAMENT ON THE UDDER

registered herds and in herds of progeny test cooperators using a linear scoring system. Twenty-one of the 23 characteristics analysed are on a linear score of one to nine. Mammary system and an overall type rating are scored on a 1 to 15 basis.

Again analysis is done using the BLUP system and it makes allowances for age at classification, dam classification, and herd classifier effects as well as information from relatives.

Traits assessed include stature, angularity, muzzle width and pin set. Apart from teat placement and the medial or centre ligament there is conjecture as to the economic benefit to be gained by selection for type traits. It must be remembered that the greater the number of traits that are selected for, the less will be the genetic progress made in any one particular trait.

Comparing Australian and Overseas Proofs

There are no valid direct comparisons between proofs of different countries. This is because different methods of analysis are used to obtain proofs and because the zero base point varies from country to country.

The ADHIS has developed a conversion method for Holstein and Jerseys for proofs from the USA, Canada and New Zealand. These rely on common sires used in all countries. These conversions—ABVs—are not perfect and have a lower reliability than ABVs. This is because some bulls perform above expectation whilst others perform below expectation. There is no way of telling what a bull will do until an actual ABV is obtained from his daughter's performances.

Recommended Breeding Programs

Most herd improvement organisations around the world recommend that of the cows suitable for breeding replacements, approximately half should be mated to the highest ranking proven sires (assessed on their total fat plus protein) while the remaining half should be mated at random to young bulls from the organised progeny test teams. This method has generally proved to be the best way of maximising genetic progress and minimising risk at the lowest possible cost.

Selection Strategy for Proven Bulls

Production pays the bills. Therefore, always select for bulls with the highest total protein plus fat rating. This is the best indication of an animal's ability to turn grass (and concentrates) into food edible by humans.

It is advisable to select a number of bulls rather than one. This minimises the chances of inbreeding in later years. Secondary selection should be based on test percentages and workability traits.

With the exchange of semen taking place between various progeny testing schemes international proofs are a possibility within a few years.

BULL PROVING TEAMS. The use of unproven bulls such as those in bull proving teams may seem risky. However, in practice, the only risk in using bulls from bull proving teams is when a limited part of the team is used. In these cases there is a risk that an unlucky person may use the worst few bulls of the team. This does not occur when a large part of the team is used.

AB centres assemble teams of young bulls for the various breeds by mating 'super sires' to elite cows.

The super sires are today's top proven sires. Sire analysts aim to get approximately eight sons of each top sire into bull proving teams over a number of years. Two or three of these sons can be expected to be substantially superior to the super sire, about half can be expected to rate the same or just above the sire and the rest just below.

The elite cows are the **top producers** of their herds and are carefully selected for type traits, reproductive performances and depth of pedigree. For an elite cow, depth of pedigree means having a proven sire and proven grandsire. This gives a much greater chance of the cow passing on her superior milk producing genes to her progeny.

ELITE COWS ARE MOSTLY FROM PROVEN SIRES AND GRANDSIRES AND HAVE WELL ABOVE AVERAGE PRODUCTION PERFORMANCE.

Time Scale for Proving Bulls.

Age of bull	Event
9 to 15 months before birth	A contract is arranged for mating or embryo transfers to be carried out on elite cows using semen from super sires.
5 months	Young bulls enter the AB centre after health testing and on-farm approval by the breed society classifier.
1–1½ years	Semen is collected and used in cooperating herds which are enrolled in a production recording scheme. The bulls are mated, at random where possible, to the cows nominated for the scheme, and care is taken to ensure that each bull is equally represented. A minimum of six cows should be nominated in each co-operating herd.
2–2½ years	Progeny are born and positively identified.
4–5 years	Daughters calve and commence lactation.
5–6 years	Lactations finish and the results are analysed to produce the ranking on each bull according to the production of his progeny.

Bulls with very high ABVs are kept as proven bulls and the best of these—the super sires—are used to breed sons for new bull proving teams. Their semen is sold widely—as many as 100,000 doses or more from one super sire may be sold. Bulls whose ABV ratings are lower are sold for slaughter. Usually only a small number of bulls makes it as proven sires, and even fewer as super sires.

Beef Bull Selection; Performance Recording and Analysis

Traits of economic importance cannot be assessed accurately by visual means. Conformation, show ring performance, coat colouring and patterns may be important at times but they give little indication of a bull's ability to transmit to his progeny the traits of economic importance (i.e. the traits for beef production).

There is considerable debate in both the scientific and commercial sectors of the beef cattle industry as to the relative importance of the various productive traits. There is a consensus of opinion, however, that for tropical areas environmental adaption outranks all other traits. Apart from this, reproductive performance or fertility is invariably the next most important trait in all environments.

The relative importance of other traits will vary according to circumstances. These traits include growth rates, temperament, structural soundness (which is not the same as show ring conformation), food conversion ability and various carcass and meat traits such as tenderness, meat composition (i.e. fatness), carcass yields and dressing percentages.

Meaningful selection to improve any trait can occur only if the trait being selected for can be measured objectively, easily and accurately and is heritable (i.e. inherited from parents) to a degree that allows genetic progress to be made.

Some of the traits of beef production have moderate heritability and allow objective measurements to be made accurately. Traits such as growth rate are easily measured whilst others such as the various carcass traits have so far only been accurately measured when animals are slaughtered.

Traits such as temperament and structural soundness, cannot be measured objectively or accurately or easily at this stage. Traits for environmental adaption and resistance to both external and internal parasites are still too difficult to measure.

Beef Performance Recording Schemes

Because growth rate is easily, accurately and objectively measured it was the first productive trait used for scientific selection of beef cattle production.

Initially performance was given as a daily or weekly weight gain. Later, performance ratios were calculated. This was done by calculating the average adjusted weight of the group to rate as 100 so that all animals are rated as a percentage above or below this base according to their individual weights adjusted for age.

There are three major disadvantages of performance ratios:

1. No valid comparisons can be made between animals born in different years, so genetic progress is impossible to measure.
2. Animals born at certain times of the year tend to be either advantaged or disadvantaged because of seasonal effects.
3. The results are expressed in terms of plus or minus. This means that half the group is always rated as a minus. This causes confusion and is resented by many cattle breeders.

These limitations have been overcome by the use of BLUP technology, similar to that used by the Dairy Industry for obtaining ABVs for dairy sires.

This technology allows valid and accurate comparisons of animals' genetic merit to be made regardless of the year or season in which the animals are born. For the Australian beef industry this process is referred to as 'Breedplan'. The genetic ratings for the various traits are called EBVs (Estimated Breeding Values).

Breedplan

Breedplan is the world's most accurate and advanced system of selecting breeding cattle on their genetic merit. Animals selected on Breedplan are more likely to pass on to their progeny the ability to perform better. On average, twice the gains available by using performance ratios can be made using Breedplan analysis. This is because analysis takes into account the performance of all known relatives of an animal as well as its own performance.

EBVs are calculated by averaging the data from the first 200 records for each trait recorded to give a herd base average of zero. Animals are rated plus (+) or minus (-) relative to this herd base according to their adjusted performance.

A bull and cow each with a +20 kg rating for final weight will **on average** produce offspring that are 20 kg above that herd base average. Obviously, by selecting breeding stock with the highest EBVs cattle breeders will obtain the best performing progeny.

GENETIC PROGRESS. Genetic progress (producing better performing animals) is made by selecting breeding stock with the highest EBVs and culling as many as possible with lowest EBVs. By continuing this process, after several generations the current herd average EBV will be well above the herd base average (rated as 0) and the animal with the lowest EBV in the herd could have a positive EBV rating.

Genetic progress is measured by comparing the herd average with the herd base average (refer to figure 60).

Group Breedplan: Comparing Animals from Different Herds

Breedplan is primarily designed for within herd comparison because each herd has a different herd base average. This means that herds on different properties within a breed cannot be compared using Breedplan, nor can herds of different breeds.

Different herds of the same breed can be compared in **Group Breedplan**. At least one common sire must be used in the herds that are to be compared. The common or link sires must have enough progeny in each herd being compared to allow valid comparisons to be made. Approximately 30 progeny by one or more link sires are the minimum required.

WIDELY USED AI BULLS ARE USEFUL 'LINK SIRES'.

The more link bulls used and the more progeny each bull has, the more valid the comparison will be. Artificial breeding programs are the only practical way of achieving Group Breedplan. By widespread use of link sires in artificial breeding it is possible to identify the top sires within most breeds throughout Australia and overseas. In these circumstances the breed base average is based on the first 200 records within Group Breedplan. (Individual herd EBVs should not be compared to Group Breedplan EBVs because the herd base averages used for individual herds will be different from the Group Breedplan base.)

The results of Group Breedplan are published each year by participating breed societies in their annual sire and dam evaluation reports.

SELECTED BRAFORD SIRES ON A STUD PROPERTY IN CENTRAL QUEENSLAND. QUALITY SIRES SUCH AS THESE ARE IDENTIFIED USING BREEDPLAN.

Traits Measured by Breedplan

EBVs are available for growth traits, fertility traits and some carcass traits.

GROWTH TRAITS. Growth traits give EBVs for birth weight, weaning or 200 day weight, yearling or 400 day weight, final or 600 day weight. Also given is a milk rating (how well a bull's daughters' calves grow according to how much milk they receive from their mothers). These growth EBVs are all stated as kg+ or kg– depending on whether they are above or below the herd or breed base average.

To assess and analyse growth rates properly, accurate birth dates are required (to at least within one week and preferably to within one day) and the animals must be weighed at least twice in their lifetime. The more weighings, the more accurate the analysis.

To assess the performance of known relatives (for more reliable EBVs), accurate pedigree information is essential. This means that individual sire mating groups and accurate 'mothering up' for dam/calf identification is essential. Management modifications may be needed in some cases.

FERTILITY EBVS. Fertility EBVs are expressed in two ways:

1. SCROTAL SIZE

The direct or male fertility rating is expressed in scrotal size EBVs. The rationale for this EBV was developed by CSIRO research which demonstrated that bulls with bigger testicles sire daughters which are more fertile. Scrotal size EBVs are expressed in centimetres above (cm+) or below (cm–) the zero base average for the herd or the breed and adjusted to a certain age (usually 400 days). Serial measurements must be taken for accuracy, starting at 10 to 14 months and finishing at 24 months usually. Again the more measurements taken, the greater the accuracy. Scrotal size is moderately heritable.

2. DAYS TO CALVING

The indirect or female fertility is expressed in days to calving EBVs i.e. whether a bull's daughters return to service and conceive after calving sooner or later than the herd or breed base average. Bulls with daughters which conceive earlier (and are hence more desirable) have a negative EBV, those whose daughters conceive

BULLS GET A DAYS TO CALVING EBV FROM THE TIME THEIR DAUGHTERS TAKE TO CONCEIVE AFTER CALVING.

later (and are hence less desirable) have a positive EBV for days to calving.

These two traits are highly correlated. Bulls with positive scrotal size EBVs will tend to have negative days to calving EBVs (so bulls with big testicles produce daughters which mature and go in calf easlier and earlier, and return to service and conceive sooner after calving).

3. GESTATION LENGTH EBVs

Although gestation length is not a measure of fertility as such, it has an influence on days to calving EBVs. Short gestation lowers the days to calving EBV as well as being an important trait in its own right.

Gestation length is the time between conception (usually considered to be at, or six hours after, mating) and birth. Accurate mating dates—such as those from an artificial breeding program—are needed for this analysis. The text book bovine gestation is 283 days but some breeds are shorter on average (e.g. Angus at 281 days) whilst others such as the European breeds are longer (e.g. Simmental at 286 days).

Shorter gestations (i.e. negative gestation length EBVs) are desirable because they allow females more time to get back in calf in time to have one calf each year. Also shorter gestations are usually associated with lower birth weights and hence less calving trouble (see 'Using EBVs for Beef Production', below).

Gestation length is moderately heritable.

CARCASS TRAIT EBVs. Ultrasonic real time scanning has allowed objective measurement of some carcass characteristics replacing the traditional methods of visually selecting for muscularity or obtaining carcass data on slaughtered progeny. EBVs are available for fat depth, eye muscle area and yield.

Fat Depth

EBVs for fat depth are calculated from scanning at the P8 site on the rump and at the 12/13th rib. They are expressed in millimetres (mm). Positive (+) fat depth EBVs indicate that a bull's progeny will be fatter (and generally finish earlier) at a given age and weight than the progeny of a bull with the herd or breed base average of zero. Conversely negative (-) EBVs indicate a bull's progeny will be leaner (and generally later to finish) at a given weight and age. High fat EBVs may be correlated with lower yield EBVs.

Eye Muscle Area

Eye muscle area (EMA) EBVs are obtained by scanning at the 12/13th rib and are expressed in square centimetres above or below the herd or breed base average.

There is considerable debate in the scientific and commercial sectors of the beef industry as to the value of EMA EBVs. EMA EBVs have an influence on yield EBVs.

Yield

There are two yield EBVs—ETMY (Estimated Total Meat Yield) and EMY% (Estimated Meat Yield Percentage). They are calculated using growth rate, fat depth and EMA EBVs.

ETMY EBVs are expressed in kilograms. This trait is highly correlated to growth rate and measures the total weight of meat produced by an animal. Fast growers produce more meat.

High yielding carcasses have large eye muscle areas and minimal fat.

EMY EBVs are expressed as a percentage of carcass weight. They are closely correlated to fat depth and EMA EBVs. High EMA and low fat EBVs lead to an increased EMY percentage.

Unfortunately high EMY percentage is negatively correlated to growth (i.e. continued selection for increased EMY percentage leads to production of smaller (but higher yielding) cattle which produce less total beef (i.e. ETMY).

OTHER CARCASS AND MEAT TRAITS. Consumer perception of meat quality comes from a number of factors. The most important of these is tenderness. Juiciness and flavour are the next most important. There is a genetic component for these traits. Other meat quality traits such as meat and fat colour and pH are mainly indicators of animal and carcass treatment and have less of a genetic component.

TENDERNESS

Although the major influences on tenderness are age at slaughter, pre-slaughter stress and carcass chiller treatment, there is a small genetic component. At this stage there is no easy, accurate or totally objective method of measuring tenderness.

JUICINESS AND FLAVOUR

The characteristics of juiciness and flavour in meat are influenced by tenderness and by the amount of fat within the meat—especially intramuscular fat. Visible intramuscular fat is called marbling.

There is a trade off between health issues and meat flavour. The Australian Heart Foundation recommends that Australian consumers should have meat containing from 3·0% to 7·3% fat. Above 7·3% fat, health issues are important and many Australian consumers regard the meat as too greasy. Below 3% fat, meat is too dry and unappetising.

Although the Heart Foundation in the USA recommends similar fat levels, many overseas customers require meat with higher fat content. The Japanese market pays a premium for highly marbled meat—meat with a high intra-muscular fat content. Fat levels over 20% are not uncommon.

Marbling has a genetic component and may be selected for. This information is not yet available in Australia but is available for some overseas sires.

Using EBVs for Beef Production

The choice of breeds and of individual bulls to be used in a beef breeding program will be determined by local environmental conditions and by the markets being targeted for supply. The selection rule—cows for the environment and bulls for the market—is still a good guideline.

ENVIRONMENTAL ADAPTION. At this stage there are no EBVs for external or internal parasite resistance, however certain breed societies (e.g. Belmont Red) do produce some tick resistance data. Perhaps the most practical method is to assume that the animals which perform the best in the harsh environments without treatment (e.g. dipping for ticks) are the best adapted or most resistant or have sufficient resistance so that production is not too adversely affected.

GROWTH. Growth rate EBVs are important because it is desirable to have animals reach target weights for the various market segments at as young an age as possible. Meat from younger animals is more tender than meat from older animals.

Selection for growth must be tempered by its effect on other traits. One of the consequences of successfully selecting for growth is that birth weights have gone up. Growth starts at conception and high growth rate is highly correlated with high birth weights. In poorly planned programs this may led to an increase in dystocia (i.e. calving or birth difficulties). Because of this adverse affect on fertility some breeders may need to compromise on growth slightly and use lower birth weight (and usually hence lower growth rate) sires to avoid trouble. Low birth weight–high growth rate sires are rare and hence more expensive. They are usually short gestation length bulls (i.e. negative gestation length EBV bulls).

One other consequence of selection for growth alone is that EMY EBVs (i.e. yield as a percentage of carcass weight) fall slightly even though ETMY EBVs will rise slightly. Yield percentage is of concern to processors more than to cattle producers. For every one per cent rise in EMY percentage there is an extra 150 t of meat available for a processing works (or feedlot) with a yearly throughput of 50,000 steers.

CARCASS AND MEAT TRAITS. Selection for carcass and meat traits again must be balanced with the effects on other traits. Selection for excessive muscling will have negative effects on growth and fertility whilst increasing carcass yield percentages. Breeds which marble well are often those with lower growth rates.

Selection of bulls for fat depth EBVs will vary according to the target market for the progeny and the cows to which the bull will be mated. Local trade markets demand earlier finishing cattle whilst the heavier carcasses required for export markets require cattle which are larger framed and heavier before maturing and finishing (depositing fat).

FERTILITY. There are no known negative correlations for selecting for fertility. Some such as scrotal size EBVs are positively correlated with growth rates (high scrotal size EBV bulls are usually high growth rate bulls).

CONDUCTING AN AB PROGRAM

Oestrus Detection Methods

Oestrus, or heat, is the period in the reproductive cycle when the cow will permit mating. Accurate detection of oestrus is the most important part of an AB program. Irrespective of the competence of the inseminator, the facilities available and the condition of the cows, the artificial breeding program will fail if cows are inseminated at the wrong time.

Personal observation is the most accurate and reliable method of heat detection available. The majority of artificial breeding program failures can be traced to nutrition and inadequate heat detection.

Visual Signs of Oestrus

The most obvious and useful sign of oestrus is mounting behaviour.

Oestrous behaviour usually occurs in the following stages:

1. The first indications of approaching oestrus are that the cow may appear restless. Some cows may appear aggressive and butt other cows, others may bellow frequently. Some chin resting may occur.
2. A short time later the cow attempts to ride other animals, particularly if none of the other cows attempt to ride her. These cows will often display signs of sexual interest—nosing other animals, smelling them, nose wrinkling, grunting before mounting and frequent dribbling of urine.
3. As the cow gets nearer to ovulation (the fertile stage) she will stand still while other cows mount her. Stages 2 and 3 are not definite but merge gradually. So cows early in heat will stand occasionally but mount frequently; cows later in heat mount occasionally but stand to be mounted quite frequently. It is best not to inseminate a cow unless she has stood to be mounted at least once. Dairy cows display this mounting behaviour quite often and visibly while beef cattle, especially *Bos indicus* cattle, mount far less frequently. As a cow passes the standing phase she may indulge in mounting of other cows.

It is not uncommon for cows which are approaching the last third of pregnancy (i.e. six months plus) to display mounting activity.

This is due to a hormone change caused by a slight regression of the corpus luteum.

4. Clear stringy mucus often covers parts of the legs and tail. Large amounts may hang in strings from the vulva. This may be particularly evident when inseminating. Uterine massage stimulates contraction, which will force mucus out of the tract. In the early stages of heat the mucus is watery. In later stages it turns stringier and thicker. (If the cow has ovulated, blood will appear in the mucus.)

Other signs of impending heat that should be watched for include:

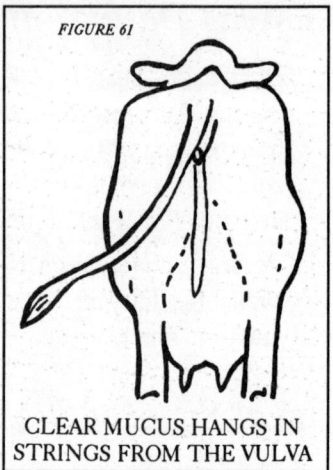

FIGURE 61

CLEAR MUCUS HANGS IN STRINGS FROM THE VULVA

- The vulva becoming swollen, wet and flabby.
- In some cows, becoming restless and being unusually alert, craving companionship and bellowing. They may walk along fence lines, urinate frequently and hold their heads up and tails to one side.
- Hair on the base of the tail being rubbed and abrasions appearing on the pin bones and base of tail. In wet weather, mud being left on flanks and hips from the dew claws of mounting cows.
- Dairy cows showing fluctuations in milk production and changes in temperament.

Despite all claims to the contrary it's not yet possible to consistently conduct successful artificial breeding programs without visually detecting oestrus in cows in the program. Mechanical methods of heat detection and oestrus synchronising drugs make heat detection easier and reduce time taken but *cannot successfully replace visual detection*.

GUIDELINES FOR VISUAL HEAT DETECTION. Follow the guidelines below when carrying out visual heat detection.

TIME

A minimum of one hour per 100 cows per day should be spent visually observing heat behaviour in the cows. The longer the time spent observing, the better the results.

TIME OF THE DAY

British breed *Bos taurus* cattle display signs of heat best at or around sunrise and sunset. This is most convenient for dairy cattle breeders as heat detection routines create no extra management duties because cows are handled at these times for milking.

Beef cattle breeders will need to adopt special management procedures. Breeders of *Bos indicus* cattle should even consider extra observations apart from sunrise and sunset as many *Bos indicus* animals do not display signs of heat as readily as *Bos taurus* animals.

A night time observation (usually after midnight), by spotlight or torch, can be quite useful for *Bos indicus* cows in addition to the normal morning and evening observations. Hotter daylight temperatures reduce visible displays of oestrus behaviour. The majority of *Bos indicus* cows commence cycling at night.

IDENTIFICATION

Every animal included in an artificial breeding program must be *individually identified*. This can be done with large double sided ear tags, freeze brands, paint brands or any other method that makes it possible to identify an animal from a distance for the duration of the program. Large paint brands on the ribs (so that other cows' mounting activities do not rub the brand) are the most practical. Both sides must be painted. The brand may need touching up during the program.

A PAINT BRAND MUST BE LARGE ENOUGH TO BE VISIBLE FROM A DISTANCE.

FREEZE BRAND

EAR TAGS

The greater the number of animals in the program, the more critical is individual identification. Problems are unavoidable with heat detection of any mob or herd over 100 cows. (Beef breeders may find it easier to do a series of smaller concise programs than one large unwieldy program.)

RECORDS

Good records are essential (see the next chapter). Whatever occurs during your artificial breeding program, write it down. Dairy farmers with a herd calving all year round will find 'heat sheets' extremely useful. Beef breeders usually find a pocket notebook the most convenient. Good records assist in **all** facets of management especially with pregnancy status of cows.

LOCATION

The actual place where you observe the cows for signs of heat is almost as important as when you observe them. Paddock observations are more useful than observations in small confined yards, providing the cattle are not too scattered. Signs of heat are most easily seen when cattle are gently pushed into mobs. Violent disturbances make meaningful observations impossible. Most accurate detection occurs when cows are relaxed. Generally, dairy observations present no problems as most dairy cows are intensively grazed and are used to being handled. Careful planning is needed for most beef situations (refer to 'Oestrus Synchronisation', below).

Mechanical Methods of Detection

Mechanical means should be used only as aids to detection. They are **not** meant to replace visual observation. They are best used in combination with visual signs.

HEAT MOUNT DETECTOR OR (HMD)

The 'Kamar' Heat Detector is a device which can be glued on the midline of the cow's back between the hip bones. Sustained pressure, from the brisket of an animal which is mounting the standing cow, squeezes dye from a compartment. A 3 second standing period is needed before dye is released.

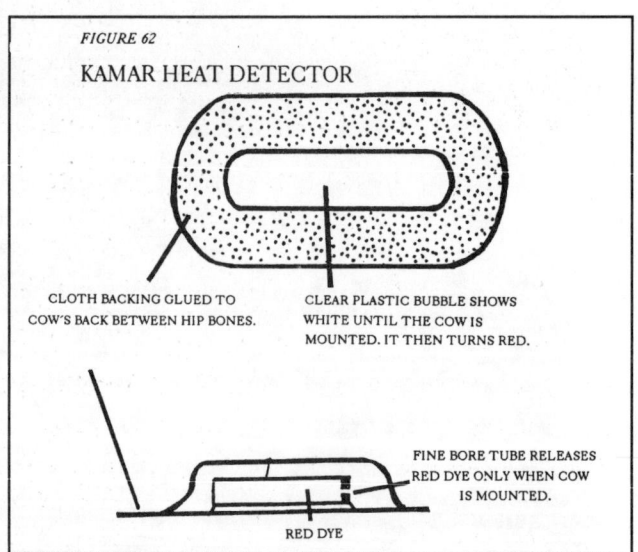

FIGURE 62
KAMAR HEAT DETECTOR

CLOTH BACKING GLUED TO COW'S BACK BETWEEN HIP BONES.

CLEAR PLASTIC BUBBLE SHOWS WHITE UNTIL THE COW IS MOUNTED. IT THEN TURNS RED.

FINE BORE TUBE RELEASES RED DYE ONLY WHEN COW IS MOUNTED.

RED DYE

The positioning of the pad will depend on the size of the cow to which it is fitted and the size of her herd mates who will mount her to trigger it. Bigger cows need the Kamar pad placed near to the tail head. (Removal of the pad must be treated as a positive sign, because they are often lost with sufficient mounts.)

The advantage of HMDs is that they are visible from a distance and do not require interpretation for results as do tail paint or chin ball harness marks.

Their disadvantages are that:

- pads may dislodge, especially in areas where cows rub on trees due to irritation caused by buffalo fly or ticks
- the adhesive may cause irritation and dermatitis
- there may be false positives
- application of the pads requires handling and labour
- extremes of weather may cause faulty operation—hot humid weather causes absorption of moisture and resultant spotting may lead to false positives; extremely cold weather may cause the dye to turn to gel.

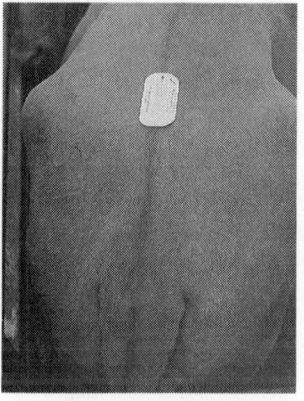

A KAMAR HEAT DETECTOR WHICH HAS NOT BEEN TRIGGERED

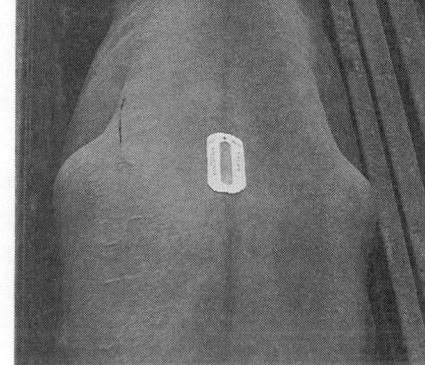

A TRIGGERED KAMAR DETECTOR IS VISIBLE FROM A DISTANCE.

CHINBALL HARNESS

This device can be attached to a teaser by an adjustable headstall. An oil-based 'ink' is contained in a stainless steel tank under the animal's chin. Cows on heat are identified by long streaks of ink on the back and rump left by the teaser dismounting.

If correctly interpreted, chinball marks are a very good indicator of a cow's sexual activity. They are particularly useful when used on 'clean up' bulls to determine which cows have conceived to the artificial breeding program and which to the clean up bull.

Chinball harnesses also have disadvantages:

- A teaser has to be used (see the comments on teasers, below).
- The teaser may resent the harness and attempt to remove it. Give the animal a

few weeks to become accustomed to the equipment before filling it with ink.
- There may be false positives, especially in yard situations with very active teasers.
- Ink may need frequent replacement with very active teasers.

A CHINBALL HARNESS ON A TEASER ANIMAL.

TAIL PAINT

Using commercially available brands of tail paint, a 'plaque' of hair and paint approximately 20 cm long and 3–5 cm wide can be painted over the butt of the tail. This can best be done by painting both against and with the 'grain' of the hair on the tail. A thick plaque is needed.

This plaque lasts for a number of weeks under most conditions, unless disturbed by the mounting action of another animal. If the cow is mounted, the plaque will turn to powder and disappear leaving only a ring of coloured hair.

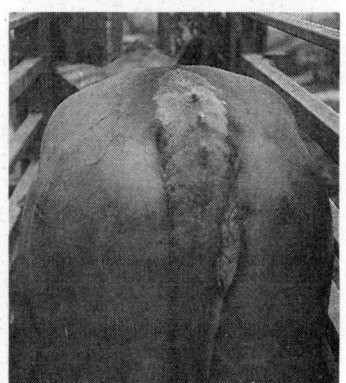

TAIL PAINT—A THICK PLAQUE IS NEEDED.

Tail paint disturbances however need to be 'read' and accurate interpretation of results may need considerable experience. Tail paint signs are not as definitive as Kamars. The advantage of tail paint is that it is inexpensive. Different colours can be used e.g. one colour to identify cows cycling before commencement of the program, another during the program, and still another to see which cows cycled after the program.

TEASERS. Teasers are animals (usually male) used to detect heat in the females of the herd. They should be sterilised or incapable of service, and are mostly used in conjunction with mechanical heat detection aids (especially chinball harnesses). There are various types of teasers:

CAPABLE OF SERVICE

Teasers which are capable of service are capable of spreading the venereal diseases of cattle (see the section on diseases in the chapter 'Factors Affecting Reproduction'). Their use is not recommended in cases where venereal disease is a risk.

Vasectomized bulls. By removal of part of the vas deferens (vasectomy) a bull is rendered sterile. Bulls may remain fertile for up to 3 months after the operation, due to sperm stored in the tract.

Cryptorchid bulls. A cryptorchid (or rig) is a bull in which one or both testes are retained in the abdomen. The retained testis cannot produce viable sperm but produces the male hormone testosterone which maintains libido. Any descended testicle must be removed (castrated) to ensure sterility.

'Souped-up' steers. Libido is induced in castrated males by testosterone injections. Repeated injections are needed to maintain hormone levels. This can be expensive.

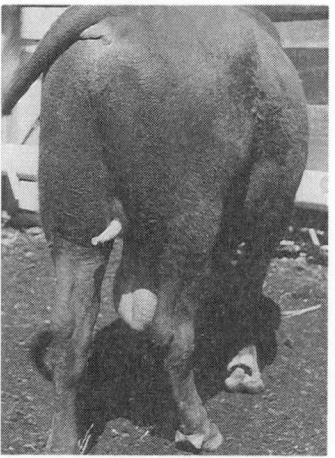

A DEVIATED PENIS OR BACKWINDER.

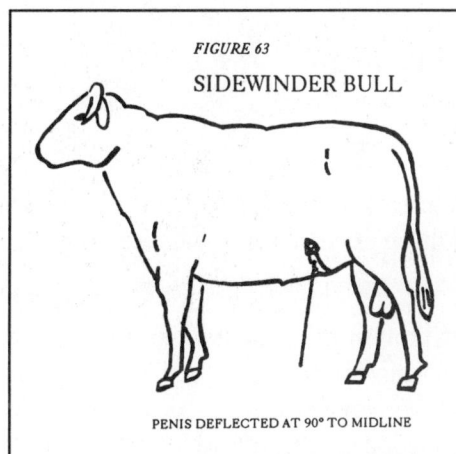

FIGURE 63
SIDEWINDER BULL
PENIS DEFLECTED AT 90° TO MIDLINE

INCAPABLE OF SERVICE

Teasers incapable of service are not a venereal disease risk.

Sidewinder bulls. The penis is transplanted from the midline to the flank so that it protrudes at right angles to the body. In most circumstances these are the best teasers to use.

Nymphomaniac cows. Cows with cystic ovaries will actively seek out all cows on heat. These cows are generally a nuisance in most herds.

Deviated penis or **backwinders.** With these the penis is redirected back to under the tail. Many of these animals suffer sunburnt penis and get infections causing them to lose interest in detecting cows on heat.

MISCELLANEOUS TEASERS

An apron may be placed in front of the sheath on a normal bull to prevent service. This is risky as it does not always remain in place.

Small bulls thought to be incapable of reaching a cow for service may also be used. This is a risky procedure.

Summary

Teasers should be used only where absolutely necessary. Breeders of *Bos indicus* cattle generally use teasers more than breeders of *Bos taurus* cattle, because *Bos indicus* cows do not display obvious signs of heat as readily.

Teasers are unproductive animals utilising feed, water and space that could be used by a breeding animal. To maintain peak efficiency, teasers must not be overused; they should be rotated frequently.

Oestrus Synchronisation

Oestrus synchronisation involves the treatment of cows so that all or most will display oestrus and ovulate within a very short time of each other.

Labour, feed and inseminating skill are required over an extended period with conventional programs. Drugs can now be used to concentrate the inseminating program to a few days. The need for oestrus detection has not been eliminated, only concentrated and shortened. There are two basic methods of bringing all cows to the same stage in the oestrous cycle:

- prolonging the luteal phase.
- terminating the luteal phase of a cow's reproductive cycle.

Prolonging the Luteal Phase

USE OF LUTEINISING HORMONE. Treatments containing luteinising hormone extend the life of the corpus luteum. This method is uneconomical and is not practical for commercial use.

USE OF PROGESTERONE Application of progesterone treatments to a group of cows over a number of days has the effect of blocking oestrous activity. On ceasing the treatment, the oestrous cycles of the cows tend to recommence in a synchronised manner with oestrus and ovulation occurring within two to six days. In the past, fertility rates with this method at the first oestrus were variable and often low. 'Silent heats' (ovulation without oestrus) were common. Low conception rates with some treatments were thought to be from 'aged ova'.

These problems have been overcome with the development of slow release depots of progesterone and by combinations with other hormones such as oestrogen, FSH and prostaglandins. Cows are usually treated with these synthetic progesterone compounds for between seven and sixteen days (nine to ten days is most common). They are usually administered by either intravaginal tampons or subcutaneous implants.

Intravaginal tampons come in two brands—'PRID' (Progesterone Releasing Implantation Device) and 'CIDR' (Controlled Internal Drug Releasing Device). They are inserted into the vagina of the cow with a special applicator. Attention to hygiene is essential for best results.

OESTRUS SYNCHRONISATION 89

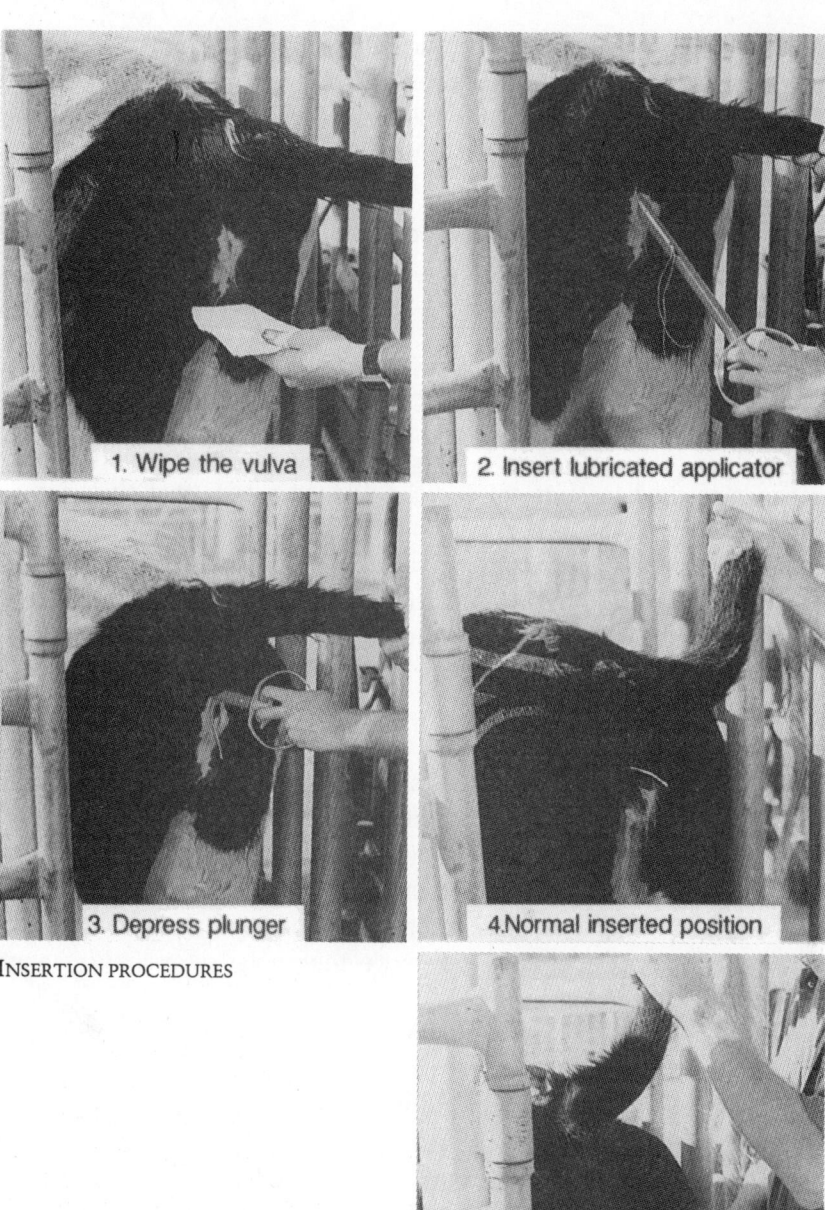

INSERTION PROCEDURES

Subcutaneous implants are marketed under the trade name of 'Crestar'. It is recommended that these be administered as an ear implant with a special applicator. (The 'Compudose' applicator is ideal.) They are removed between nine and eleven days later. Injection into the fold at the butt of the tail is not recommended.

The following features of PRIDs, CIDRs and Crestar are worth noting.

- These products are 'safer' for both cow and operator than the other method of synchronisation using prostaglandins (see below). All can be safely handled by the operator without side effects and will not cause abortion if accidently administered to pregnant cows. Crestar is an S4 scheduled poison and has to be obtained from a veterinarian. CIDRs and PRIDs may be bought over the counter.
- These products tend to start cows cycling which means that they are more suitable for cows in poor reproductive condition than are prostaglandins. However, artificial breeding programs should only be attempted using cows in known **sound breeding condition**. Artificial breeding programs on anoestrus cows fail regardless of drug company claims.
- Administration and removal of these products require more handling of cows than some prostaglandin programs.
- PRIDs and CIDRs may cause vaginitis to appear in some cows—seen as a pus discharge. Generally it does not affect subsequent fertility during the artificial breeding program but may be disconcerting to the inseminator. Because of it, hygiene is essential when inserting intravaginal tampons.
- Crestar implants must be administered carefully between the skin of the ear and cartilage. A good head bail and nose grips are essential. Sometimes the ear may have to be nicked with a scalpel to remove the implant. *Bos indicus* animals greatly resent this treatment.
- PRIDs, CIDRs and Crestar are generally more expensive than prostaglandins, especially when used in combination with other drugs.
- The manufacturers often claim that inseminations at a set time after removal of the synthetic progesterone can be used for a successful artificial breeding program. According to these claims, the cows can be blanket inseminated 48 or 56 hours later with no heat detection. This may not always work under most conditions, and it is strongly advised that these products be used to control heat detection time, rather than to eliminate heat detection.
- Crestar is not to be used on dairy cows which are lactating or on beef cattle for slaughter. The withholding period is a minimum of 52 days. This is because the progestagenic action of Crestar is strong enough to affect human reproduction.

Terminating the Luteal Phase

This can be done by manually expressing the corpus luteum during a rectal examination or by use of a luteolytic agent such as prostaglandins. Manual expression of the corpus is not recommended as it is a very messy procedure which can cause adhesions and bleeding, leading to reproductive problems.

PROSTAGLANDINS. Prostaglandins are naturally occurring luteolytic agents, (i.e. they dissolve the corpus luteum) which are released in the body between Days 17 and 19 as part of the normal oestrous cycle of a cow (see the chapter 'Physiology of Reproduction of the Cow'). Some synthetic prostaglandins also have this luteolytic action and are used extensively for oestrus synchronisation.

Only cows in the luteal phase of their oestrous cycle will respond to prostaglandin therapy. On average, 60–70% of a group of normally cycling cows are in the luteal phase (that is, between Days 5 and 19) at any one time. Responding cows will come on heat two to four days after treatment.

Cows not in the luteal phase are unaffected by prostaglandins. The most commonly used prostaglandins are Estrumate, Lutalyse and Prosolvin. All are given as IM (intramuscular) injections. (Lutalyse as a 5 cc injection, Estrumate and Prosolvin as 2 cc injections.)

There is a number of ways in which prostaglandins may be successfully used to synchronise cows to come on heat. However, before administering prostaglandins to any cows, much planning is needed to ensure that the drug will work as expected. The following points should be noted.

- Prostaglandins are not fertility drugs. If used correctly they will neither increase nor decrease fertility. Their use is to control the times that cows comes on heat. This can be arranged to suit the inseminator and to simplify heat detection.
- Prostaglandins will only work properly on cows which are cycling normally. Non-cycling cows generally do not respond (i.e. do not come on heat at the desired time.) Cows in poor condition, cows losing weight and those just recently calved, are most likely to be non-cyclers and hence poor respondents. Cows which are pregnant less than five to six months **will abort** if treatment with prostagladins is attempted. Cows over five to six months pregnant may not abort but should not be treated.
- Prostaglandins are **dangerous to humans** if accidentally administered. The use of prostaglandins is strictly regulated, they are S4 scheduled poisons, and they should only be used under the supervision of a veterinarian. They should not be handled by pregnant women, asthmatics or people with glaucoma.

PROGRAMS FOR PROSTAGLANDINS. Start planning 1 year ahead (refer to the section on planning, below). Check *every* cow or heifer in the program. Each must be empty and cycling for prostaglandins to work. Use only cows that have calved at least six weeks previously. Cows can be checked to see that they are cycling by the use of tail paint or by pregnancy testing by a veterinarian. Temporary (false) weaning may assist in getting cows to cycle after calving. If maiden heifers are used, they must also be checked for cycling activity and pregnancy

There are several ways to use prostaglandins successfully.

The ten day program. This is the most cost effective method of using prostaglandins.

- **Step 1**   Day 1 to Day 5—observe and inseminate cows on signs of heat as per a normal observation program.
- **Step 2**   Day 5—inject with prostaglandins all cows which have not demonstrated signs of heat or been inseminated.
- **Step 3**   Day 6 to Day 10—observe cows and inseminate them on signs of heat. Large numbers of cows will respond to the injection on Days 7, 8 and 9, with the odd animal still responding on Day 10.

N.B. Some cows will come on heat at Day 6; these will be cows that did not respond to the injection but came on heat naturally.

A cattle breeder considering using prostaglandins should use the ten day program before any other because of the following advantages.

- In built safety factors. The cycling activity of cows is checked for in the five days before prostaglandins are administered. If cycling activity is less than expected, i.e. less than 4–5% per day (on average), the program can be abandoned.
- Heat detection and insemination routines can be polished up in the first few days prior to the larger numbers of cows all coming on heat together from the synchronisation. Large numbers of cows all on heat at once are hard to detect accurately.
- Minimal amounts of drug are required but the program is still shortened markedly enough to be worthwhile.
- The results obtained are optimal. Although prostaglandins do not increase fertility rates, many cattle breeders report success rates above those that could otherwise be expected, because heat detection efficiency is so much improved due to the concentration effect of synchronisation. Dairy farmers find this program most useful when inseminating maiden heifers; their results are usually excellent.

The 2/2 program. This program includes two injections with prostaglandins and two 'blanket' inseminations, so it involves no heat detection.

- **Step 1**   Day 1—inject all cows with prostaglandins.
- **Step 2**   Day 11—inject all cows a second time with prostaglandins.
- **Step 3**   Day 14—inseminate all cows.
- **Step 4**   Day 15—inseminate all cows again.

The 2/2 program is designed to *eliminate* the need for heat detection. In theory, the second prostaglandin injection should synchronise all cows. In practice, the results are extremely variable because of different responses to the second injection and because of a spread of ovulation times. This is the most costly program for drug and semen usage, and is not recommended.

A variation of this program is to heat detect the cows on Days 13, 14 and 15 and to inseminate only those cows which have been detected displaying oestrus. This is far more efficient than blanket insemination but often overall success rates are still very low.

The intermediate program. This program attempts to combine the minimal costs and higher conception rates of the ten day program with the minimal labour and heat detection effect of the 2/2 program.

    Step 1   Day 1—inject all cows.

    Step 2   Days 3, 4 and 5—observe, and inseminate on signs of heat.(Approximately 60–70% of cows should respond and be inseminated.)

    Step 3   Day 11—inject for a second time those cows which did not come on heat.

    Step 4   Days 13, 14 and 15—observe, and inseminate on signs of heat. The bulk of the remaining 30–40% should be picked up.

This program is probably the most suitable for beef breeders inseminating large numbers of cows although, on average, the results are not as good as those obtained from the ten day program.

SYNCHRONISING PROGRAMS USING PROGESTERONES. Like prostaglandin synchronisation programs, synchronising programs using progesterones should be planned 1 year ahead. Use only those cows which are empty and have calved at least six weeks previously, so that they are cycling (refer to the section on planning, below). The major differences in conduct of progesterone synchronising programs from prostaglandin synchronising programs are:

- Synchronisation is much tighter. Up to 100% of cows will respond and show signs of heat within two to three days compared with 60–70% on prostaglandin programs. This means that there is no polishing up time for heat detection and insemination practice such as that which occurs in a ten day prostaglandin program
- Extra handling of cattle is needed for administration of drugs and removal and for the extra drugs needed to be administered to ensure good results.

CIDR AND PRID PROGRAMS. There has been a number of different programs devised for synchronising using CIDRs. The most recent and successful is as follows:

    Day 1   Administer CIDRs to the cows by insertion into the vagina, with careful attention to hygiene.

    Day 6   Administer by injection a dose of prostaglandins. When using CIDRs with capsules this may not be necessary or a one-half dose of prostaglandins only may be given.

    Day 10   Remove CIDR.

Start heat detection 36 hours after removal of the CIDR. Detect heat for three days. Inseminate normally, following the a.m.–p.m. rule (see page 51δ). If necessary, cows may be treated with FSH to help ensure that ovulation occurs. This is preferably done on Day 9 (one day before CIDR removal) but may be done at CIDR removal on Day 10.

Some CIDRs may have attached oestradiol capsules. These aid luteolysis. CIDRs with capsules are an S4 scheduled poison and have to be obtained from a veterinarian.

CRESTAR PROGRAMS.

Day 1   Cows are treated with the Crestar ear implant which contains a synthetic progesterone (Norgestomet) and at the same time are given an injection containing the synthetic progesterone and oestradiol (for luteolysis).

Day 9   Cows are treated with FSH to help ensure ovulation. (This is sometimes done on Day 10 but is not as effective then.)

Day 10   The ear implant is removed.

The procedure recommended by the manufacturer of Crestar is to inseminate a set time after removal: 48 hours for heifers and 56 hours for cows. A safe alternative is to commence heat detection 36 hours after removal and inseminate on signs of heat. Continue heat detection for three days.

Planning and Preparation

In a successful artificial breeding program, a dose of fertile semen is placed in the correct position in the reproductive tract of a normal, healthy cow in good nutritional condition, at the right stage of the breeding cycle. It sounds simple but none of these things will occur by accident and advanced planning is essential. Failure of an artificial breeding program is usually due to lack of preparation and poor management, not the inseminating ability of a technician.

The first step is to determine the type of artificial breeding program to be attempted.

1. **Continuous observation.** This is the type of program for dairy farmers on a 'year round' calving pattern. The cows are observed twice daily for most of the year. A beef breeder would not normally consider this type of program.

2. **One cycle program (21 to 28 days).** Twenty one to 28 days is the time necessary to allow each cow in the program to cycle once. The cows are observed twice daily for 21–28 days. These programs are conducted mainly in beef areas where feed and/or labour is a limiting factor, and in some dairy herds with strictly seasonal calving.
3. **Two cycle program (42 to 45 days).** This system requires twice daily observations for 42–45 days so that all cows have the chance to cycle twice. It allows some cows to be given a repeat insemination. It is used sometimes for beef herds and often for seasonally calving dairy herds.
4. **Part herd program.** This type of program is implemented when only a portion of the herd is to be inseminated. For instance, you may have only 40 doses of semen, but a herd of 200 breeding cows; the first 40 cows demonstrating oestrus will be inseminated. In this case the program should take only four to five days. It is this type of program which is most common in very extensive beef situations if herd bulls are being bred.
5. **Synchronised programs** (described above). These make it possible to inseminate large numbers of cows in a short time.

SUCCESSFUL ARTIFICIAL BREEDING PROGRAMS. The success of an artificial breeding program is expressed theoretically in the result of this formula:

$$\text{Bull fertility} \times \text{inseminator efficiency} \times \text{cow fertility} \times \text{heat detection efficiency} = \text{calves on the ground}$$

The individual components in order of importance are:
1. heat detection efficiency
2. breeding soundness of the cow, i.e. cow fertility
3. efficiency of the inseminator
4. fertility of the semen, i.e. bull fertility.

HEAT DETECTION EFFICIENCY

This is the critical factor in most AI programs. The most skilful inseminator in the world using the most fertile semen available cannot get cows in calf unless the cows are presented at the correct time for insemination. It is in this area and in the area of cow fertility that most of the advanced planning must be done.

Heat detection efficiency depends on:

Skill and experience. Normal cow behaviour must be known so that small changes in behaviour can be recognised and interpreted.

Time spent. A minimum of one hour per 100 cows per day must be spent on oestrus detection. Early morning and late afternoon are the best times as cows do not demonstrate signs of oestrus as strongly in the hotter parts of the day.

Because they concentrate the timing of heat detection, synchronised programs are very useful in most beef situations.

Size of the herd. In all situations the accuracy of detection declines as cow numbers increase. This is especially so when more than 100 cows are in a program. For this reason it is better to run a number of smaller concise programs than one large unwieldy program. Synchronised programs are ideal in this respect.

Facilities and paddock yards. Small paddocks are preferable to large ones. Heavily timbered, hilly or rough paddocks are to be avoided. The ideal is a number of smaller open paddocks with adequate shade and water, used in rotation. These paddocks should be as close as possible to the yards and insemination area. Synchronisation programs again are very useful because they reduce the time during which cows have to be fed.

Ease of identification of cows. All cows must be ear tagged or have large visible fire, freeze or paint brands. Poor identification is the most common reason for cows being missed or the wrong cows being presented for insemination. Each cow must be easily identifiable from a distance. Tag or brand cows before commencing the program.

Heat detection aids. Even with the closest observation some cows will not demonstrate oestrus visibly. Heat detection aids such as heat mount detectors and tail paint may assist in identifying them, but these are only aids and should not be used instead of observation.

In a well managed program, 80–90% or more of the cycling cows can be detected.

Cow Fertility

The organisation and selection of cows to include in an artificial breeding program must be planned in detail for all types of programs except those utilising continuous observation, i.e. dairy farms calving all year round.

Only cows which are capable of going into calf should be selected for a program. Selection of suitable cows is best achieved by a per rectum examination of the reproductive tract by a veterinarian. Animals which are not cycling or which show signs of reproductive tract infections or abnormality should not be chosen. The major reasons for rejecting cows from a program are:

Pregnancy. This occurs due to lack of control of one's own or one's neighbour's bulls, i.e. poor breeding management. Poor record keeping will make the problem worse. **No cow** should be treated in any way to synchronise heats unless she has been pregnancy tested.

Reproductive tract infection. This may be detected upon veterinary examination or when insemination is attempted. If the incidence is more than 1–2% of cows, seek veterinary advice.

Anoestrus (non-cycling). The major reasons for non-cycling (apart from pregnancy) are poor nutritional status and stress. Cows which are losing weight or even just maintaining their body weight have a much higher incidence of anoestrus. The majority of cows cycle strongly when they are gaining between 0·25 and 0·5 kg per day (see the section on nutrition in the chapter 'Factors Affecting Reproduction'). Cycling activity can be checked using tail paint. Tail paint all cows and place in the program only those with paint removed. Alternatively, experienced veterinarians or owner inseminators can select cycling cows by ovarian palpation while pregnancy testing.

First calf cows. Cows calving for the first time are generally not suitable for inclusion in an artificial breeding program as they are still growing, may be losing teeth and the shock of the first calf may delay the recommencement of cycling activity.

Miscellaneous reasons. Other factors affecting cow selection include age, time since calving and the lactation status of the breeders. Wet (lactating) cows are more likely to exhibit anoestrus. The suckling of calves will often induce 'lactation anoestrus'. The more times the calf suckles a cow, the greater is the chance that the cow will remain in anoestrus. Cows on poor nutrition and first calf cows (heifers) are most affected. Temporary weaning, early weaning and/or supplementary feeding may help overcome lactation anoestrus. Temporary weaning—removal of calves from cows for 24–48 hours—is generally sufficient to induce cows to recommence cycling. Do not include cows in the program that have calved less than six or seven weeks previously. Old cows and cows with poor temperament are less likely to conceive and should be culled. All cows used in the program should be tested free of the reproductive diseases.

Remember that every dud cow in the program means extra work for provision of feed, heat detection, drafting, etc. Check all the cows before the program and use only those which are likely to be fertile. A really well managed program should have 90% or more sound breeders.

INSEMINATOR EFFICIENCY

Inseminator efficiency is measured by the ability to hygienically place the dose of semen in the correct place. Correct semen handling is *vital* and depends on **proper facilities.**

Technical competence. Only people who have had adequate training should be attempting an AI program so most of the faults in technique will be due to complacency and not to incompetence. Poor facilities cause anxiety for the inseminator and the cow, resulting in poor restraint and poor insemination technique. The insemination crush should be approximately 1·5 m long and 66 cm wide. It should have a concrete floor for hygiene and to minimise wear.

ADEQUATE RESTRAINT FACILITIES ARE ESSENTIAL.

FACILITIES NEED NOT BE ELABORATE—JUST PRACTICAL WITH A COVERED INSEMINATION AREA.

The crush and its surrounding area must be roofed. A head bail is useful but should only be used in extreme cases. Restraint of the cow and safety of the operator can be achieved easily with a britching chain (Tindall chain) or backing gate. Squeeze bails or crushes are capable of the most complete restraint of any animal. Animals requiring such restraint procedures are generally not suitable for most artificial breeding programs.

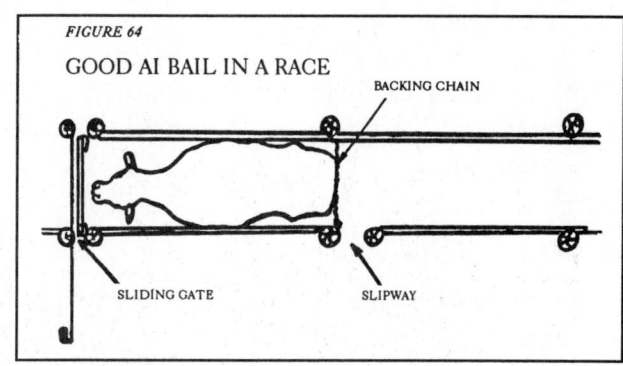

FIGURE 64
GOOD AI BAIL IN A RACE

The type of squeeze bail shown in the photo is excellent for use on unhandled cattle. (The one shown is from Hughenden Welding Works, in use in an artificial breeding training school.)

Timber yards and crushes are preferable in some cases to steel, as the noise made by steel facilities will upset the cows unless they are worked through the yards regularly. *Nervous and frightened cattle will not go in calf as easily as quiet cows.* Where possible, water should be laid on at the yards, for washing equipment and for settling dust if necessary.

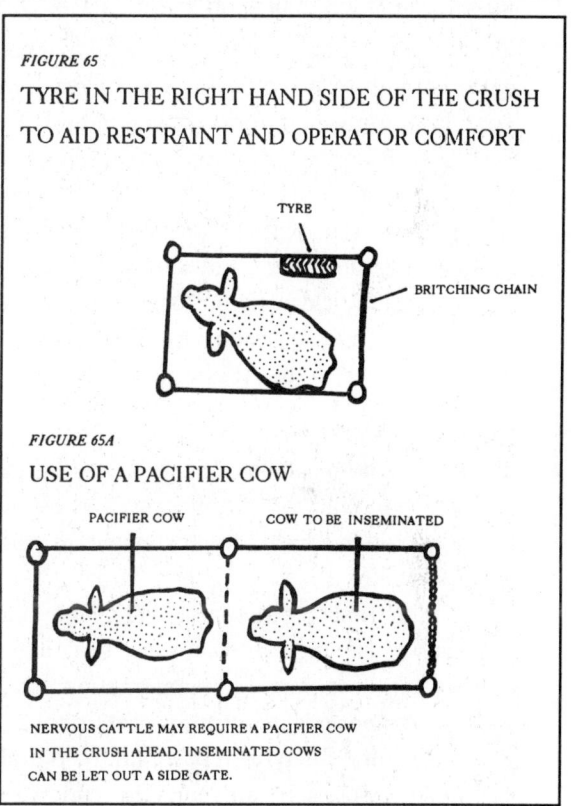

FIGURE 65
TYRE IN THE RIGHT HAND SIDE OF THE CRUSH TO AID RESTRAINT AND OPERATOR COMFORT

FIGURE 65A
USE OF A PACIFIER COW

NERVOUS CATTLE MAY REQUIRE A PACIFIER COW IN THE CRUSH AHEAD. INSEMINATED COWS CAN BE LET OUT A SIDE GATE.

In a normal program, using adequate facilities, inseminator efficiency should approach 100%.

BULL FERTILITY

When purchasing semen, always buy from licensed AB centres or licensed distribution centres. Non-recognised centres do not always maintain strict quality standards.

Some bulls have a naturally lower conception rate than others. Licensed AB centres test the fertility of their bulls and adjust dilution and processing to raise the conception rates of the lower fertility bulls. Each straw of semen sold by the recognised AB centres is capable of fertilising a cow when sold. Any deterioration in fertilising capability of the semen is due to poor handling and loading procedures. For this reason bull fertility should be assumed at 100% for most circumstances.

Clean Up Bulls

Some managers turn the whole herd out with bulls to settle those cows which did not conceive in the artificial breeding program. These 'clean up' bulls should be introduced at a rate of approximately 1%.

This is quite a good practice provided that the artificial breeding program is started early enough to avoid having the calves from natural service drop too late in the year. Sometimes a different breed of bull is used to differentiate between artificial breeding and natural service calves. Otherwise, you can delay putting in the clean up bull for one heat cycle (i.e. 3 weeks) and when the cows subsequently calve down, check the calving dates very carefully so that the artificial breeding calves can be separated from the clean up bull's calves. Alternatively, put a chin ball harness on the clean-up bull and check cows daily to see which cows are marked and when. You can assume that cows which are not marked but do calve down have conceived to the AI program.

SUMMARY OF PLANNING STEPS.

1. Check the feasibility of the planned program. There must be definite reasons and benefits for attempting a program. Consider whether these can be achieved more easily and cheaply by other methods.
2. Determine the best time to attempt the program. Consider the availability of feed and labour; the farm work load; and existing animal husbandry practices such as calving patterns, weaning times, etc. to see if these will be compatible with the program's implementation. Also avoid times of environmental stress such as periods of extreme heat or cold.
3. Determine the type of program to be undertaken.
4. Make provision for suitable paddocks to house the breeding herd for observation. Consider paddock location and size, shade, feed and water. If supplementary feeding is needed, order it or provide it ahead of time. Cows should be fed sufficiently so that they are gaining weight for six weeks before and six weeks after the program, to ensure maximum calf drop.
5. Select and identify cows to be included in the program. Work them through the yards to get them into a routine. Tag cows *before* commencing the program. Only those with maximum conception chances should be included. *Select the cows and plan the feed up to one year ahead*.
6. Check the restraint facilities *before* the program starts.
7. Order equipment, semen and nitrogen *before* it is required. Leave precise delivery instructions with the AB centre. Delays can be costly. Ensure that

sufficient equipment, semen and nitrogen are on hand and make provision for rapid resupply if necessary.
8. Have clean up bulls on hand (one bull per 100 cows) at the completion of the program if required.

BREEDING RECORDS—THE BASIS OF SOUND MANAGEMENT

FIGURE 66
SOUND MANAGEMENT DECISIONS ARE BASED ON GOOD RECORDS.

A profitable herd is the sign of a good manager. Sound management decisions are based on good records. Breeding records are more than just a history of calving and mating dates. They make it possible to keep a close eye on the performance of *each cow*, as well as the herd as a whole.

Lost profits and added costs occur because of:

- empty cows
- extended intercalving intervals
- too many days open
- failure to breed
- anoestrus.

To get rid of the deadwood in your herd you need a record of what each cow is doing. Reproduction is just as important as production. In terms of profitability in the dairy industry, a cow's performance in getting into calf is just as important as her performance in filling the bucket. In the beef industry no calf means no income from that cow.

Breeding Performance Standards for Dairy Cattle

Litres of milk per day indicate a cow's production standard. Breeding records allow measurement of each cow's reproduction performance. These records identify cows which are having difficulty meeting breeding performance standards.

Breeding performance standards are based on the management aims for the herd. Common breeding performance standards for dairy herds are for each cow to:

CALVE EVERY TWELVE MONTHS.

It is desirable to have cows calving every twelve months to allow the calving pattern of the herd to be structured around the seasonal feed availability and market milk requirements. If too many cows calve outside the twelve month period this pattern will be disrupted.

FIGURE 61

Fresh cows convert feed into milk. Stale cows tend to put it on their backs. Smaller, fresher herds (i.e. calving regularly) can produce the same amount of milk as larger staler herds (i.e. with less regular calving).

CONCEIVE WITHIN 83 DAYS AFTER CALVING

To calve every twelve months a cow must conceive within 83 days after calving. As a cow's reproductive tract takes up to 42 days to recover from calving, conception must occur in the relatively short period between 42 and 83 days after calving. Most cows, if given the chance, can be mated successfully in this period.

CYCLE WITHIN 42 DAYS OF CALVING

Even though the reproductive tract is still returning to normal, most cows should cycle within 42 days after calving. Keeping a record of all heats after calving will identify cows which are unable to cycle. These are potential difficult breeders or problem cows. With early attention many of these cows can be pregnant by 83 days.

NEED LESS THAN THREE MATINGS

Most cows hold to their first or second service. Cows needing more services can be a particular nuisance. Intercalving intervals are longer and the cost of inseminating is higher. These problem cows often suffer from infections of the uterus or disorders of the ovaries. Most of them can be treated successfully if treated early enough.

HOLD TO SERVICE

Complete heat records allow a more accurate confirmation that a cow has held to service. All too often, empty cows reach the dry paddock.

HAVE A NORMAL PREGNANCY

Interruptions to normal pregnancy, i.e. abortions, should receive particular attention. They may be due to reproductive diseases such as vibriosis or leptospirosis which can easily be spread to the rest of the herd.

HAVE AN ADEQUATE DRY PERIOD

A rest on good feed after lactation, to build up body reserves, can have a positive influence on a cow's ability to milk and to get in calf next lactation. Sixty days is considered ideal.

Problem Cows

Signs which serve to identify problem cows include:
- being empty
- showing no signs of heat
- not holding to service
- having too many days open
- having abortions.

Problem cows are those not meeting the standards set by most of the herd. They are a source of lost profits and added cost and they are often very hard to identify.

FIGURE 68

CULL PROBLEM COWS

CAUSES OF PROBLEM COWS. Dairy cows have stresses, and problem cows have more than their share. Records should identify the symptoms of stress and a bit of detective work may identify the cause. Dairy veterinarians conducting 'herd health' schemes are particularly useful in this area.

Symptoms

SHORT TERM	LONG TERM	POSSIBLE CAUSES
Inhibited ovarian activity (i.e. no heat)	Long periods empty (extended periods between calving)	Poor condition at calving Loss of condition after calving
Inhibited conception (need for returns to service)		Infections caused by difficult calving or retained afterbirth
Pregnancy not completed (abortions)		Infection of the uterus Cystic ovaries Old age Youth (of first-calf heifers) High production Suckling calves Reproductive diseases External and internal parasites General diseases (e.g. tick fever, three day sickness) The cow may be suffering from a combination of stresses

Farmers will also be stressed because they will have stale cows and lower profits.

SOLUTIONS. Some solutions are easy—extra feed in the bails is all that many problem cows need. Remember, prevention is generally cheaper than cure. Once you have detected a stress, try to minimise its effect in future.

Other solutions are not so easy—a good manager is always ready to seek professional advice. The local vet can treat most problems, and usually the cost of professional treatment is far less than the loss of profits sustained by unproductive cows.

Practical Breeding Records

A recording system is only as good as the information which is put into it. To be effective the system must be:

- updated daily—information not put in is lost or forgotten
- checked regularly—checking once a month will show trends and allow accurate early decisions to be made
- simple—information must be easy to put in, easy to take out, easily understood and meaningful.

Complete farm breeding details can be kept on two records: working records and permanent records.

WORKING RECORDS. Working records are designed for day to day decisions on breeding management and have two facets of operation.

(a) They act as a history of recent events such as:
- heat dates of each cow
- mating dates with sire and dam identification
- calving dates with sire and dam identification
- drying off dates
- treatment
- other important events.

(b) They act as a predictive calendar for events such as:
- expected calving dates
- expected drying off dates
- expected heat dates
- expected feed requirements for certain parts of the year.

Recording all heats makes it possible to detect problem cows early and gives a reasonably reliable indication of pregnancy status.

Working records are designed to focus attention on those parts of the herd due for:
- mating
- calving
- drying off or pregnancy testing.

Commonly used working records include:

Heat sheets. These are calendars based on the average cow's 21 day heat cycle. They are very useful for the predictive facet of working records, especially in detecting problem cows. Details such as calvings, matings and treatments can be recorded at the bottom of the sheet.

Shed sheets. Cows are recorded on these sheets as they calve, or in alphabetical or numerical order. Calving details, mating details, treatment details, etc. are recorded under the cow's identification. These sheets may also contain information from the previous year.

Wall calendars. These are 365 day circular plastic or wooden calendars. Days are represented by a series of holes around the outside of the calendar and cows are identified by pegs (in colours for calving, mating, drying off). Performance standards are marked on the wall behind the calendar (e.g. 83 days calving to conception, 300 day lactation, etc.) and the central calendar can be moved to check on individual cow performances.

Simple pocket diaries. These are very useful when some time may elapse between seeing the cows and entering the details in a more permanent record.

Cow card index. Each cow's history is recorded on an individual card, and cards can be arranged in order of calving or in alphabetical or numerical order. This system is also very suitable as a permanent record. However, details are not easily read and cards tend to suffer when in constant use as a working record.

PERMANENT RECORDS. Permanent records are used to enable long term selection decisions, on a genetic or production grounds. Information kept on permanent records includes:

- Cow identification including pedigree and birth date (to fix the cow's age).
- Details of breeding history including mating dates, sires used, calving dates, identification of calves and the fate of calves.
  Details of production history including the number of lactations, drying off dates to fix lactation length, individual production recordings, total lactation production, and total lifetime production.
- Treatments, diseases and the eventual fate of the cow.

Commonly used permanent records include:

- a cow card index
- an exercise book—with one or two pages per cow
- computers.

Complete records of all facets of farm operations can now be kept simply on computers. Computers are becoming comparatively cheaper each year and many farmers now use them. There are commercially available software packages suitable for most dairy farms. Veterinary herd health and other commercial organisations offer computer facilities for many dairies

Breeding Performance Standards for Beef Cattle

The degree of detail needed to be kept in beef recording systems will vary. Bull selling enterprises such as studs (and AB centres) have to supply extremely detailed information, but most normal commercial enterprises can function efficiently with simple records.

A calf or carcass from each breeding cow each year is a realistic aim for all beef enterprises. To achieve this, individual cow numbering is essential. One simple system, which allows one hundred new breeders each year to be brought in and still recorded with only three characters each, is to make the year letter the first character and use numbers for the other two. P24, for example, identifies the twenty fourth heifer born on the property in 1994—which is year "P" in the NASIS year code sequence (see the chapter 'Semen—Collection, Processing and Storage').

Many commercial beef operators would use 424 to identify the same heifer using the 4 of 1994. This system works quite satisfactorily providing cows are culled for age at ten years. Using the year letter cows may be kept longer without confusion.

Information Recorded

Basic information such as cow identification and pregnancy status may be all that is needed in some commercial enterprises. Additional information such as individual performance, temperament and reasons for culling can all be placed on simple computer spreadsheets or in an exercise book.

More detailed records are needed (e.g. for Breedplan analysis) by bull selling enterprises. Detailed individual performance data and progeny performance data are required. Data of this detail must be kept on individual cow cards or on commercially available computer programs. Data for each cow should include:

- cow identification
- date of birth
- detailed pedigree
- number of calves
- mating details
- actual date (or time of exposure to bull)sires mated with
- calving details
- dates
- difficulties
- birth weight of calves
- performance details
- EBVs for growth and milk
- progeny performance details
- weaning weights
- yearling weights

- scrotal size of male calves
- eye muscle area details

Some breed societies allow a linear scoring system for conformation similar to that used in dairy sires, which can be reflected in the records.

FACTORS AFFECTING REPRODUCTION

Nutrition

Nutritional factors influence post-calving fertility. Body condition has a significant bearing on reproductive efficiency; cows gaining 0·25 to 0·5 kg per day are more likely to cycle and conceive than those animals which are losing condition or even just maintaining condition.

The major components of a ration are:
- proteins
- carbohydrates
- fats
- water
- vitamins
- minerals
- roughage (for 'gut fill').

PROTEINS. Proteins are a complex group of substances which are characteristic of living matter. They are essential for growth and the maintenance of body functions including reproduction. Mature native tropical and sub-tropical pasture grasses are generally low in protein, especially in winter, and unless some form of supplementation is used when grazing these pastures, body condition and reproductive performance may deteriorate. Feedstuffs which have a high protein

TROPICAL PASTURE HAS LOW PROTEIN IN WINTER

content include cotton seed or soybean meal and good quality legume hay. Urea provides the least expensive form of non-protein nitrogen supplementation. The bacteria in the rumen (paunch) convert it into protein. Licks or drum rollers with a urea-molasses solution can assist in maintaining body condition when cattle are run on low quality pasture.

There must be an adequate level of protein in the ration for the animal to utilise carbohydrates for energy production. Cattle can utilise even very poor quality pasture provided there is sufficient protein.

CARBOHYDRATES AND FAT. Carbohydrates and fat provide energy which is essential for all body functions. When animals are under nutritional stress, e.g. during lactation, energy supplementation may be required. Grain and molasses are cheap sources of energy. Energy supplementation allows more efficient use of available roughage.

HIGH PRODUCING DAIRY CATTLE NEED ENERGY SUPPLEMENTS TO MAINTAIN PRODUCTION.

Good quality pasture and crops such as ryegrass, oats, sorghum and lucerne are generally adequate in both energy and protein. Normally these are the cheapest form of supplementation available.

WATER. Water is essential at all times. Dairy cattle, when lactating, require more water than beef animals. If cattle are grazing on very lush pasture their water consumption will fall. Beef cows need up to 40 L per day whilst dairy cows need far more than this while lactating.

VITAMINS. Prolonged vitamin deficiencies are extremely rare in grazing cattle.

MINERALS. While many minerals are essential for good health and reproduction, phosphate deficiency is of most importance in Australia. It is easily recognised as

'Peg Leg' or bone chewing. Marginally deficient cattle will appear normal but will have reduced reproductive performance.

Trials in marginal phosphate areas have shown that marked increases in conception rates can be obtained by making phosphate supplements available to all breeders and growing stock. Critical periods are the last third of pregnancy and during lactation. At these times phosphorus requirements are high.

All dairy cattle need phosphorous supplementation. This boosts production as well as reproductive performance.

Effects of Nutrition on Fertility

The effects of nutritional stress during the mating period can be reduced or overcome by supplementary feeding and strategic weaning.

Supplementary feeding. This should only be undertaken after consideration of the costs and likely benefits. The strategic use of improved pasture or crops can often provide the required lift in feed quality in the most economical way.

Strategic weaning. This can be one of the most useful and economical methods of alleviating breeders from stress. Weaning time should be gauged by the condition of the breeders and the quality of feed available to them. If the cows are in good order, calves can be left on them for a longer period. If the condition of the cows is falling, calves should be weaned. Try to wean prior to winter or any prolonged dry spell. With the calves removed the breeders may at least hold condition or gain weight before calving.

Early weaning should be normal management practice in drier tropical areas. It is cheaper to feed the calves directly than through their mothers. Weaning at weights down to 150 kg should be considered in normal seasons and in emergencies, such as severe drought conditions, even lighter calves can be weaned advantageously.

Spike Feeding. In tropical areas an energy boost for a short period during pregnancy can increase the chances of the cow conceiving after calving. This does not have to be prolonged. Six to eight weeks is generally sufficient.

Early weaning or a short sharp burst of energy supplementation can be effective in boosting conception rates for subsequent matings after calving.

Diseases of Reproduction

There are four main diseases which effect the reproductive tract. **Leptospirosis** and **Brucellosis** are contagious diseases which can also be transmitted to humans. **Vibriosis** and **Trichomoniasis** are both venereal diseases which do not affect humans.

LEPTOSPIROSIS. Several strains of the Leptospira organism cause disease in Australia: *Leptospira pomona, L. hardio, L. tarassovi* and *L. icterohaemorrhagiae*. The organism is fragile and will only survive a few days outside the host. It causes a serious (but generally not fatal) fever in man. The disease in humans is known as swamp fever or tropical fever. The highest incidence of this disease in humans is found in veterinarians, inseminators, dairy and pig farmers and abattoir workers.

CATTLE CAN CONTRACT LEPTOSPIROSIS BY DRINKING WATER CONTAMINATED BY WILD PIGS.

Transmission. The organism enters hosts—horses, pigs, cattle, man, rats, etc.—by their ingestion of infected material, especially water, or by skin penetration through mucus membranes, such as those of the eyes and mouth, or through cuts and abrasions of the skin.

Leptospires localise in the kidneys and will be excreted in the urine for up to two months by cattle and pigs. Wild pigs urinating near or into the water supply are an important means of spreading the organism. Rats, bandicoots and other small animals are also common causes of transmission. Bulls rarely transmit the disease mechanically but the organism may survive in diluted semen.

Effects. About 25% of infected cows will abort, usually in the last third of pregnancy. Calves may be born weak causing high neonatal losses. There can be a high mortality rate if young calves contract the disease. Signs in calves include red water (haemoglobinuria) and sudden death. (Calves rarely get red water from tick fever.) Cases of abortion occurring during wet periods may often be associated with the introduction of infected animals. These abortions are not normally followed by retained membranes.

Diagnosis. Blood tests at a laboratory to determine antibody levels and type of organism present.

Control. Routine vaccination of breeders and of calves at four to ten weeks of age is recommended in suspect areas. Blood tests will have to be performed to determine which vaccine should be used. Dairy cattle should be vaccinated twice a year. Once a year will suffice for most beef cattle. Drainage of low lying ground and fencing off suspicious areas may assist in control.

Treatment. Streptomycin is the best drug to use as it kills the organism and prevents excretion in the urine. Valuable cows and bulls are usually the only animals treated. In most cases antibiotic treatment is not cost effective.

BRUCELLOSIS. Brucellosis is produced by the *Brucella abortus* bacterium. It is also known as Bang's Disease or contagious abortion and can affect humans as undulant fever. The disease in humans is not normally fatal but does cause prolonged illness. It is found most commonly among veterinarians, inseminators and meat workers.

The organism is hardy and will survive for long periods in faeces, moist soil and water. Direct sunlight will destroy it. At the time of publication bovine brucellosis was considered to have been eradicated from Australia. However, bovine brucellosis is still present in other countries.

Transmission. Cows contract the disease by eating contaminated material, e.g. grass contaminated by uterine discharges or infected foetal membranes. If a cow aborts, the foetus and membranes should be burned to prevent the spread of infection. Calves can be infected by drinking contaminated milk. Bulls can act as carriers of the disease and can transmit the organism through semen.

Effects. The disease is characterised by late abortions, i.e. in the last three months of pregnancy. Early abortions can occur if a susceptible cow becomes acutely ill.

The organism localises in the uterus and invades the placenta. This disrupts the supply of nutrients to the foetus causing it to weaken or die. Some aborted calves may live for a short time but they usually die soon after.

Because of the involvement of the placenta, foetal membranes are often retained after calving or abortion. This is particularly so if abortion occurs after five months. Retained placenta often leads to pyometron (pus in the uterus) or metritis (inflamation of the uterus). Both conditions can cause infertility.

Diagnosis. Laboratory tests on blood, milk or seminal plasma.

Control. Test and slaughter of infected animals.

VIBRIOSIS (Campylobacteriosis)

This is a venereal disease. The organism cannot live outside the genital tract of the cow or bull.

Transmission. The disease is spread by infected animals mating with clean ones.

Artificial insemination with contaminated semen may also transmit the condition. If not treated, bulls remain carriers but cows will develop an immunity. Young bulls are less susceptible to infection than older bulls.

Signs. Often the only sign of the disease is reduced herd fertility. Mid-term (five months) abortions may occur. There can be a marked drop in conception rates if an infected bull is introduced into the herd. Because of early embryonic deaths, infected cows show irregular returns to service. Detailed records such as those kept by well managed dairy farms are needed for diagnosis by records.

Diagnosis. Collect samples of vaginal and preputial mucus for laboratory diagnosis.

Control. Artificial breeding eliminates vibriosis as infected cows develop immunity and clean cows will not be contracting the condition. Vaccines are available and these are quite effective with young breeders. They may leave unsightly lumps at the site of injection.

Treatment. Bulls—vaccination is the most effective and preferred treatment but a preputial douche of penicillin and streptomycin in peanut oil, ten minutes daily for three consecutive days may be used. Cows—intra-uterine infusion with streptomycin and penicillin can be attempted. This is expensive. Most cows will develop a natural immunity and breed normally after six to twelve months.

TRICHOMONIASIS. This is a venereal disease caused by the *Trichomonas foetus* organism. It is not transmitted to man.

Transmission. The disease is spread by infected animals mating with clean ones. The organism will only survive in the reproductive tract. The bull's glans penis and prepuce seem to harbour the greatest concentration of the organism.

Signs. Frequently the only sign is reduced herd fertility. The disease causes early abortions, at four months pregnancy and under. This is seen as irregular and lengthened oestrous cycles. The embryo may not be expelled when it dies. There may be complete re-absorption and in some cases pyometron. Purulent discharges may be seen. In some cases mummified foetuses will remain in the uterus.

If the penis of the bull is affected it will appear inflamed.

Diagnosis. Preputial and vaginal mucus samples can be cultured in a diagnostic laboratory.

Control. Management and artificial breeding.

Treatment. Seek veterinary advice. As a general rule animals should be culled.

USES OF ARTIFICIAL BREEDING

The demand for a product or technique depends on how useful it is and what advantages it offers. Artificial breeding offers many advantages to prospective users. The disadvantages are purely technical and future developments should eliminate them.

Advantages of Artificial Breeding

AVAILABILITY OF PROVEN BULLS. Proven bulls are the most important advantage of artificial breeding. Progeny testing is the most trustworthy assessment of a bull's worth. AI allows quick and accurate progeny testing. Progeny testing or 'Bull Proving Schemes' give dairy farmers access to proven bulls which have demonstrated their ability to improve herd production. For beef cattle, bulls with Breedplan figures should be used where possible. AI provides the cheapest and simplest method of obtaining link bulls for Group Breedplan.

A TOP DAIRY SIRE MAY HAVE 100,000 OR MORE PROGENY.

AI IS THE EASIEST WAY TO GET 'LINK BULLS' FOR GROUP BREEDPLAN.

READY ACCESS TO GOOD BULLS. Without AI the grazier or dairy farmer had to be content with commercial herd bulls. Now top bulls are within everyone's reach. Each bull standing at an AB centre is there because he has one or more characteristics of benefit to the industry. These characteristics may have been assessed through eye appeal, pedigree, show ring successes, the bull's own performance or his progeny. No individual could own all the donor sires available at AB centres, but they are available to any producer able to use an AI service.

AI ALLOWS FARMERS ACCESS TO BULLS WHICH THEY COULD NOT AFFORD TO PURCHASE.

MAXIMUM USE OF SUPERIOR SIRES. Under natural service conditions a top sire could be expected to sire about 200 calves in his lifetime. With AI the same sire is able to produce up to 500,000 calves in the same period, and his use can extend after his death. Consequently, an AB sire can have a great beneficial impact on the industry.

DISEASE CONTROL. Provided AI is the only breeding method used, it eliminates venereal disease (vibriosis and trichomoniasis). Artificial breeding, as such, has little effect on the incidence of brucellosis and leptospirosis. However, because using AB demands closer attention to herd management, including better record keeping, opportunities for disease control are better in herds where it is used.

IMPORTATION OF NEW BREEDS AND BLOODLINES. Under our existing quarantine regulations, the importation of livestock from most overseas countries is prohibited. Similarly, semen importations are tightly restricted. However, it is physically easier to transport semen and embryos than live animals.

Through importation, producers have been able to enjoy the benefits of the exotic breeds such as the Charolais, Chianina, Simmental and Limousin. New bloodlines of the well established breeds such as the Hereford and Holstein-Friesian can also be introduced.

This, of course, can work both ways and Australia is able to export semen overseas.

INSURANCE AGAINST UNAVAILABILITY OF SERVICE THROUGH DEATH OR INJURY. Owners of valuable bulls can have the bulls' semen collected and stored to preserve their genetic material. This is often cheaper than insuring against the bull's death or injury, and his genetic material remains available no matter what happens to him.

Should some disability prevent the bull from mounting, semen can still be collected by the electro-ejaculation technique and processed normally. However, it is important to ensure that this disability is not a genetic factor which would be passed on to the progeny.

INTANGIBLE BENEFITS.

Reduced need to keep bulls. It may be possible to eliminate the need to keep bulls particularly on small, intensive properties. This limits the frequency of accidents associated with bulls. Property management can also be improved, as fences can be maintained better and more economically.

Improved management. To maximise the efficiency of AB, accurate records on individual cows have to be kept. A beneficial side effect is the better overall herd management that results from having comprehensive individual records.

FIGURE 69
UNMANAGABULL

More uniform calf drop. A well run AI program should get a large percentage of the cows in calf in a short period. The resulting concentration of calf drop compares favourably with what can be achieved under natural service conditions, even in herds with 3% or more bulls. When methods of oestrus synchronisation are improved, an extremely uniform calf drop can be expected.

Better herd control. With artificial breeding, the breeder knows which calf came from which bull. With natural service, unless there is only one bull, there is no way of ensuring sire identity. It is possible to segregate breeders according to feed requirements if no bulls are retained on the property. If a grading-up or crossbreeding program is carried out by artificial breeding, as opposed to natural service, it is less complex. Good records work more efficiently than the best fences.

ECONOMICS. It is difficult to make generally applicable statements about the economic comparison of artificial breeding and natural service. For each cattle enterprise a separate analysis is required to work out where the economic advantage lies—and even then, it is necessary to incorporate inexact speculation about the productivity of progeny to be obtained from natural and artificial breeding. In making a cost comparison, it is important to take into account that AI programs reduce the need to invest capital in maintaining and replacing herd bulls, and enables productive cows to be run in their place, generating additional income.

As has been pointed out, few graziers or dairy farmers can afford to invest in bulls of the calibre of those maintained at AB centres. Instead of being a capital investment with continuing maintenance costs—as is the case with herd bulls—artificial breeding is a repeatable expense incurred only over the lead up period and at the time of mating.

Disadvantages of Artificial Breeding

As technology in the laboratory improves and herd management becomes more accustomed to artificial breeding, disadvantages will diminish. For example, improvements in technology allow the convenience of handling frozen straws rather than chilled semen in test tubes.

TRANSMISSION OF GENETIC FAULTS. As was pointed out earlier, an artificial breeding sire can produce several thousand progeny in his lifetime. This means that if the bull possesses a genetic fault it could be spread over a large number of progeny.

For this reason extensive monitoring of donor sires includes:
- health testing
- chromosome studies and, more importantly
- performance and progeny testing.

ECONOMICS. The economics of artificial breeding have been referred to earlier. The dollar cost of getting a cow in calf on extensive properties may be higher using artificial breeding as opposed to natural service. The logistics of handling large numbers of cattle, observing and possibly inducing synchronised heat, increase costs. Again, as technology improves some of these costs will be reduced.

ADDITIONAL SKILLS AND LABOUR REQUIRED. An artificial breeding program places additional demands on management, particularly in detection of oestrus, keeping of records, etc. However, closer monitoring of breeders produces added benefits.

REDUCTION OF STUD SALES. As more producers use artificial breeding, their demand for herd bulls diminishes and there may be a general reduction in sales. For some studs artificial breeding can be profitable, as semen rights can be sold, rather than the bull himself, and higher prices may be commanded.

RESTRICTION ON REGISTRATION. All artificially bred progeny in dairy breeds can be registered in an appropriate appendix or herdbook. Some restrictions occur within the beef breeds. No general statement can be made, as each beef breed society has its own set of regulations regarding the use of artificial breeding.

If it is intended to use artificial breeding to produce registerable stock, the person responsible for conducting the breeding program should check with the relevant breed society before starting the program.

GLOSSARY

Abortion — Miscarriage. Expulsion of the premature foetus or embryo.

ABV — (Australian Breeding Value) Measure of the genetic merit for the production traits of dairy cattle.

Accessory sex glands of a bull — Bulbo-urethral glands, prostate gland and seminal vesicles.

Acrosome — Part of the head of the sperm that carries enzymes.

Adrenalin — Hormone produced by the small adrenal glands which are situated near the kidney. Adrenalin is released in response to fright, excitement or anger and one of its effects is to slow down or stop the normal contractions of the uterus after service, thus affecting fertility.

Ampulla — Structure where the vas deferens joins the urethra.

Anoestrus — Absence of cycling. (*See also* oestrous cycle, and cystic ovary.)

Antibiotic — Chemical product derived from or produced by living organisms which is capable of preventing the growth of undesirable bacteria.

Brucellosis — Disease which causes abortion in cattle.

Bull proving — Progeny testing scheme for dairy bulls.

Capacitation — Maturing of the sperm in the female genital tract. This process is necessary before the sperm is capable of fertilising the ovum.

Cilia	Short threads projecting from the exterior of a cell, which make it move by beating.
Chromosome	Paired, thread like structures within the nucleus of a cell. Chromosomes carry the hereditary factors called genes and are present in constant numbers in each species (e.g. 30 pairs in cattle).
Conception	Union of the egg and sperm (fertilisation).
Corpus luteum (CL)	Yellow body on the ovary formed in the site of a ruptured Graafian follicle.
Cystic ovary	Ovary in which a cyst has developed due to failure of a Graafian follicle to rupture (owing to some hormonal upset) or due to the prolonged presence of a corpus luteum. These cysts may cause frequent or continuous oestrus, or complete absence of oestrus.
Cotyledons (with caruncles)	Attachment point where placenta and uterus join to exchange oxygen, carbon dioxide and nutrients.
Diluent	Material used to dilute or 'extend' the semen.
Dizygotic	Originating from two separate fertilized ova. Dizygotic twins are also known as non-identical twins.
Dominant gene	Gene which overrides the effect of the alternative recessive gene where both are present in one individual. For example, the gene for polled is dominant over the gene for horns.
Dystocia	Difficult birth.
EBV	Estimated Breeding Value. Rating of genetic merit for various beef production traits.
Ejaculation	Discharge of semen by the bull.
Electro-ejaculation	Collection of semen by the stimulation of the

	bull with an electric current passed across the accessory glands.
Emaciation	Severe loss of body condition.
Embryo	The developing calf from conception to the forty eighth day of pregnancy.
Endocrine glands	Ductless glands which produce hormones.
Enzymes	Organic solvents.
Epididymis	Sperm storage organ on the testes.
Faeces (feces)	Excrement from the bowels.
Fallopian tube	Passage connecting an ovary to the uterus.
False heat	A cow not on heat, but showing one or more of the external signs associated with heat.
Fertilisation	Union of the egg and the sperm.
Foetus (fetus)	Unborn calf, from the forty eighth day of pregnancy until birth.
Follicle	*See* Graafian follicle
Freemartin	Infertile female twin of male–female twins. In approximately nine out of every ten bull–heifer twin calves, the heifer is a freemartin.
FSH	Follicle stimulating hormone. Pituitary hormone which stimulates the growth of the follicle in the ovary.
Gametes	Sex cells—sperm in males, ova in females.
Gene	Minute particles located along the chromosomes. They are responsible for the transmission of hereditary characteristics from one generation to the next.
Gestation	Pregnancy.

Gonads	Primary sex organs—testes in males, ovaries in females.
Gonadotrophin	Hormone which acts on the ovaries or testicles.
Gn RH	Gonadotrophin releasing hormone
Graafian follicle (follicle)	Fluid filled sac within the ovary containing the egg.
Gun	Insemination pistolette.
Heredity	Transference of characteristics from parent to offspring.
Heritability	Degree to which a characteristic can be transmitted from the parent to the offspring.
Hormone	Chemical substance which regulates and maintains various functions of the body. Hormones are produced by glands and transmitted by the blood stream to their site of action.
Inbreeding	Mating together of related animals.
Infertility	Inability of a domestic animal to breed as often or as regularly as its owner would wish of a normal individual. (Compare with sterility.)
Karyotype	Orderly photographic representation of chromosomes.
Lactation	Formation and release of milk from mammary glands.
Leptospirosis	Disease which causes abortion in cattle.
Libido	Sex drive—usually refers to male animals.
Licensed semen (unrestricted)	Semen produced at a licensed AB centre and available for public sale.
Line-breeding	Inbreeding.

LH	Luteinising hormone. A pituitary hormone which acts on the ovary to stimulate the development of the follicle and the formation of the corpus luteum.
Luteolysis	Dissolving of the corpus luteum.
Luteotrophic	Promoting the growth of the corpus luteum (– with reference to compounds).
Mammary glands	Udder
Monozygotic twins	Identical twins. Originating from a single fertilized egg (zygote) which splits into two identical halves.
Nucleus	Central body in a cell controlling its activities.
Nymphomaniac cow	Cow showing marked and almost continuous signs of heat (*See also* Cystic ovaries).
Oestrogen	Hormone which is responsible for producing the (female sex hormone) signs of heat.
Oestrus	Heat (*see* Oestrous cycle).
Oestrous (estrus) cycle	Regular sequence of stages which the cow undergoes from one heat to the next. The oestrous cycle is divisible into *four* stages. 1. Oestrus—the heat or season phase of the cycle 2. Metoestrus—the phase of the oestrous cycle immediately after oestrus. 3. Dioestrus—the quiet period in between normal heat periods 4. Pro-oestrus—the phase of the oestrous cycle immediately before oestrus. Anoestrus is the non-breeding period. The period when there is no evidence of oestrus occurrence.
Oviduct	Fallopian tube–q.v.
Ovulation	Release of the egg or ovum from the ovary.

Ovum	Female germ cell; an egg cell (plural—ova).
Oxytocin	Pituitary hormone which causes the contraction of the uterine muscle.
Palpation	Examination by touch and pressure.
Parturition	Process of birth.
Penis	Male organ of copulation (plural—penes).
Pituitary gland	Important gland which produces hormones situated at the base of the brain. Part of the function of this gland is to regulate the reproductive cycle (the oestrous cycle and the production of milk).
Progeny	Offspring.
Progeny test	Evaluation of offspring to determine the genetic merit of parents.
Progesterone	Hormone produced by the corpus luteum of the ovary. It is essential for the establishment and maintenance of pregnancy.
Prostaglandins	Naturally occurring compounds which cause luteolysis. Synthetic prostaglandins are used for oestrus synchronization.
Prolactin	Hormone causing udder formation and milk production.
Purulent	Containing pus.
Scrotum	Pouch containing the testes.
Silent heat	Occurrence of ovulation without visible signs of heat.
Sperm	Male gamete or sex cell.
Spermicidal	Lethal to sperm.
Sterility	Total inability on the part of an animal to breed.

	When it is only a partial inability the term 'infertility' is used.
Synchronisation	(Of oestrous) Inducing a number of cows to display oestrus within a short time (see prostaglandins).
Testis	One of the pair of male reproductive glands, (plural-testes).
Testosterone	Male sex hormone. It is produced by the testis and induces libido.
Trichomoniasis	Venereal disease of cattle.
Urethra	Tube which leads from the bladder to the outside—opening at the end of the penis in the male and into the floor of the vagina in the female.
Venereal disease	A disease which is mainly transmitted during mating. See vibriosis and trichomoniasis.
Vibriosis (Campylobacteriosis)	Venereal disease of cattle.
Yellow body	Corpus luteum.
Zygote	Fertilized egg. A single cell structure resulting from the union of the egg and the sperm.